LICENSED TO REAR

A Novel

Riya Aarini

ISBN: 978-1-956496-49-9 (eBook)

ISBN: 978-1-956496-50-5 (paperback)

Library of Congress Control Number: 2024915877

First published in Austin, Texas, USA

www.riyapresents.com

To parents, expectant parents, hopeful parents,
not-so-hopeful parents, and someday parents

Chapter 1

One ordinary Sunday morning, Mila Winston ran her hand-held vacuum up and down the orange fur of a giant plush teddy bear, towering seven feet high—a gift from her parents and a not-so-subtle hint that they hoped to be doting grandparents soon. Not that she needed the hint. She was determined to start her family on her own distinct terms.

Mila's husband, Jason, walked in, his attention glued to his phone as he cheered on the number one tennis player in the nation during a live-streamed match. Jason never missed a game and even ate dinner with it blaring on television. She knew the man she married—including his quirks—inside and out and didn't mind.

"Hon," Mila said, without looking up from vacuuming. She kept their house clean and orderly, as she did her life. She was far from a neat freak but decided that organization was better than disorganization, care was better than neglect, and proper was better than improper.

"Uh-huh?" Jason didn't turn his gaze away from the game.

"We've been married three months."

Jason looked up. "Has it been that long? Seems like we just got married last week."

"Yes, hon, time flies when we're having fun." She turned off the roaring handheld vacuum and set it down on the beige acrylic carpet.

Her hands on her hips, Mila turned to face her husband. Serious conversations required serious stances. "I think it's time we start looking for a nice place to start our family."

"What's wrong with Peoria?"

"Hon, everything's wrong here." Mila's answer came out exasperated. Her voice escalated as she began to rattle off the multitude of dissatisfactions that irked her like a pine needle jabbing her side. "The crime rate, the lack of quality schools, the poverty. Come on, Jace, we can't raise a family here."

He scratched his head. "Uh, okay. Where then?"

Mila ran to the side of the bed and plucked a glossy brochure off the nightstand. It had been folded and curled to reveal a particular page, as if waiting to be pointed out. "See?" She set her slender index finger on a small ad at the bottom of page nineteen. "I think we should move here."

"Coolbeensia? Huh, an odd name." Jason looked off into the distance. "But I think I've heard of it before. Isn't that the place where you need a license to have children?"

Mila smiled, nodding emphatically. He'd heard of it, which eliminated the first hurdle and pushed them one step closer in the right direction. "Yep, it's perfect."

"How're we going to get a license to raise a family?" His shoulders inched up. "It's unheard of."

"But brilliant." Mila patted her husband on the arm. Naturally, he showed concern, as they'd discussed having children long before they officially tied the knot. Having a full house was important to them both. Children would complete their family, plus a furry pet or two, besides the giant stuffed bear.

"It's no biggie. It's just like earning a license to drive. You've done it before, and so have I. We'll be assured that we're surrounded by qualified parents who know how to keep their kids safe. Isn't that like what a driver's license is for?" She gazed at him, hoping her brief but logical answer would convince him.

Jason twisted his lips. "I guess." He took a deep breath and let it out. "Maybe you're right." He paused. "Come to think of it, you're always right." He looked at her sparkling gray eyes. "Where is it?"

"Well, I've read up on the literature. Coolbeensia is a tiny micronation down south. I believe it's surrounded by the territory of northwest Texas."

"So, it's in Texas but not a part of the United States?"

"Right, it's an independent nation. Though it's unrecognized by other sovereign nations, it's still a legitimate one, with its own president, military, navy, judicial system—and, most importantly, it's governed by its own laws." Laws differentiated one nation from another and made or broke its success.

Jason wiggled his head, the curious way teachers did when they heard a bright student giving a bright answer. "Eh, peculiar laws, for sure."

He wasn't getting on board as easily as she thought.

"But they're great laws." Mila's words came out nearly pleading as she tightened her arms against her chest, the magazine pages crumpling slightly and producing a crinkling sound. She gazed at her husband in his pondering moment. Maybe a wife's penetrating stare would sway him.

"What if we don't pass? Then what? I don't want to jeopardize our future family if one of us fails."

"Oh, honey, you've never failed a driver's license exam, have you?"

"Um, no."

"It can't be that hard for two dedicated would-be parents who only want the best for their future children, right?"

"I guess not." Still, Jason didn't look convinced.

Determined, Mila upped the ante.

"Plus, we're teachers. We know all about exams. We give them to our fourth graders every week. It's not a far stretch for us to take another exam."

"Yeah." His voice came out shaky.

"If it helps, dear, we're supposed to attend the Resz Parenthood Polytechnic, which is a school that prepares would-be parents for the Parenthood Competency Test, the PCT. By the way, the Polytechnic is named after Coolbeensia's esteemed president, His Excellency the President Eloney Ben Resz. He's Hungarian. Neat, huh?"

Jason's eyes glossed over.

Okay, so a president with Hungarian ancestry didn't impress him. Still, it was cool.

"Once we pass, all we need to do is be sworn in at the Office of Parenthood to show we're capable of the job of parenthood." It was simple to explain and couldn't be simpler to accomplish.

"That's a lot of steps just to be a mom and dad."

"Of course it is. That's the whole idea. But they're worth it. Think of the quality of life our children will have. We'll be among other parent professionals who care deeply about the job of parenthood."

"Parent professionals?" Jason scratched his dirty-blond hair.

She knew this was a whole new ballgame for him. Mila herself had only heard of Coolbeensia after she picked up that glossy woman's magazine at the grocery store checkout stand three days ago. But its unique laws instinctually spoke to her future maternal self.

Mila stood back, still clutching the magazine, her hands on her hips again. "Don't you see? Doctors need a license to practice medicine. Lawyers need a license to practice law. Coolbeensian parents need a license to practice parenthood."

"Ah, yeah, now I see." He sounded sarcastic.

"Sweetie, you married me, and for good reason."

He began to smile. "You are one of the smartest people I know."

A frown appeared on Mila's petite face. "One of?"

Jason laughed. "I mean, you are the smartest person I know. Sorry, slip of the tongue."

"Well, then? Don't you want to listen to the recommendation of someone who knows what she's talking about?" Mila's tone came out playfully, though she was dead serious.

"We're planning for the well-being of our future children, the little people who will one day grow up and be a part of an elementary school class, a high school, a college, and then society at large. Shouldn't we make an active effort to prepare them to be the finest individuals they can be?"

Jason whipped his head around and looked at his wife, eye to eye. "I can't argue with that."

Mila backed away, smiled, and nodded. She had him wrapped around her finger. She could feel it.

She clapped her hands, the fleeting sound breaking the stillness in the air. "It's settled then. We're moving to Coolbeensia."

"Not so fast."

Mila's frown returned and her shoulders took a slump, leaving her thin frame hunched over as if she'd had a rough day, even though it was a relaxing Sunday and she'd been full of pep just a second before.

"Coolbeensia, well . . ." Jason started, his voice trailing.

"Well, what? It's perfect. No place could be more ideal to raise a family." Tension filled Mila's voice, leaving her almost squealing like a desperate animal trying to escape a pen.

Jason rolled his brown eyes up and then over to one side. "It'd be moving to a new country, literally. Coolbeensia is an independent nation, even if it's surrounded by the territory of the United States. I'm sure we need passports. I've got to think about this. Give me a few days, huh?"

He glanced over at his wife and gave her a half smile.

His request was reasonable. She'd give him time. After all, it wasn't like she was asking him to move up north to Wisconsin, which so far remained a part of the United States.

Mila dropped her shoulders and twisted her body left and right, like a child undecided about strawberry or chocolate ice cream. "Oh, okay. It is a major life change. We'll circle back in a few days."

She pecked him on his ruddy cheek and returned to the corner of the room to straighten the tangled polka-dot bowtie wrapped snugly around the giant plush bear.

Chapter 2

Returning home after teaching on Monday, Mila began chopping red leaf lettuce, a smooth Hass avocado, and four hard-boiled eggs in preparation for a protein-packed salad. She'd make an enticing meal her husband couldn't resist. He loved her cooking, and she wasn't about to disappoint.

She grabbed a handmade, fair-trade wooden bowl, the one she and Jason had picked up from an exotic craft market during their honeymoon travels to Peru. When the opportunity arose, she made sure to support crafters who were paid fairly for their work and used wood that preserved the biodiversity of forests.

Mila tossed the chopped lettuce into it, and then the avocado and eggs. She sprinkled matchstick pieces of Swiss cheese over the heaping salad to create a presentation of stunning beauty, a feast for her husband's eyes. He was sure to be hungry after a long, eight-hour day, and an appetizing, homecooked dinner might sway him to see her side of things.

Just as she rinsed her hands under a cool stream of water and dried them on the patterned-green kitchen towel, her phone chirped.

She ran to her phone and opened up the text message. *Hmm. Jason will be late. He's got some emergency at the school.* Mila set the phone down and sighed. *Hope everything's all right.*

Five o'clock came and Mila sat down to dinner alone, squirting her chef's salad with ranch dressing and gobbling up her meal. She helped herself to garlic bread, freshly toasted with a sprinkling of chives, infusing the air with a savory scent. Mila finished her dinner with a small brownie she'd baked from a boxed mix over the weekend. Not every sumptuous dessert had to be made from scratch. Cutting corners was perfectly acceptable for a busy, working wife.

Mila plopped down on the couch and flipped on the television with the remote. She glanced up at the clock to see its short hand on the six and the long hand just past the one. Watching the boring evening news, she tried to keep her eyelids from shuttering closed. Despite her efforts, she fell fast asleep.

At eight o'clock, Mila awoke abruptly. "Jason? Jason?" She got up off the couch and peered through the curtains.

The April night had descended, ushering in a thick, gloomy darkness. His car still wasn't in the driveway. "Oh, brother, must've been a big emergency."

She climbed the stairs to the upstairs bathroom and got ready for bed.

At nine o'clock, Mila slid her legs under the thick purple reversible comforter, which kept her and her husband warm during the frigid Illinois winters, when temperatures could drop below freezing. She propped a fluffy down pillow behind her back, grabbed her tablet off the nightstand, and resumed reading where she'd left off. The light from the lamp on the nightstand gave off a warm yellow glow, but she didn't need it when she had the light from her tablet illuminating her story.

Mila sat engrossed in the unsolvable mystery with her eyes squinting and two small vertical lines appearing in the middle of her forehead, on either side above her nose bridge. Whodunnits always kept her awake into the wee hours of the night, even when Jason snored steadily next to her.

Keys jangling in the front door lock startled her. She dropped the tablet, threw off the comforter, and ran downstairs in her pink silk pajamas.

"Jason! What happened?" she asked a haggard Jason, with his white, button-up dress shirt hanging half out of the waist of his khaki pants, his hair tousled, and his posture stooped like the hunchback of Notre Dame. He'd never looked this washed out after work.

"What a day," he moaned, as he dropped his briefcase on the floor. His keys slipped out of his grip. Instead of falling into the ceramic bowl on the table next to the door, they landed outside of it with a cacophonous clank. Mila ignored the fact that the keys weren't in their proper place. She was more interested in the emergency that had kept her husband away.

"Tell me." She hurried to her husband and grabbed his arm, leading him to the couch.

He collapsed into the soft, thick brown cushions.

Mila took a seat next to him, throwing her legs onto the cushions and giving him her full attention.

"You won't believe it."

"Well? I can't believe anything if you don't explain what I can't believe."

Jason took a deep breath and gazed ahead. "Mikey, my student, fainted in class."

"Oh, why?" Students fainted for all sorts of reasons, like tiredness or heat. But it was only Monday, with the kids back from a relaxing weekend, and springtime, when they weren't exposed to the Midwest's scorching summer temps.

"First, I gave him some water. He didn't drink it, because he'd fainted. But he opened his eyes when the cold liquid splashed against his lips. He rested there, still woozy.

"I told my assistant to call an ambulance. She did."

"What made him faint?" Mila asked, her voice a near squeal.

"I'm getting to that, hon," he said, pushing his hands in front of him.

"I asked Mikey what caused his fainting spell." Jason turned to face Mila, who didn't take her eyes off him as he spoke. "You won't believe what he said next."

"What?" Mila's eyes grew big. Her grip tightened around her husband's arm.

"As we waited for the paramedics, he said his mom went to see her boyfriend on Friday night, leaving him a bag of chips and a can of soda. Apparently, she'd told him that she'd be back Monday."

Jason had a class full of nine-year-olds, like Mila did. She couldn't imagine any parent leaving a helpless child alone for an entire weekend, without supervision—and definitely not without food.

Her husband shook his head. "Poor kid. He'd eaten the bag of chips, probably snack size, for his Friday dinner. All weekend long, he had nothing to eat. The only reason he came to school this morning was for the free school lunch."

Mila's jaw dropped.

"Nine years old, alone, and starving in the land of plenty." Jason dropped his head between his knees for a minute. He straightened up and threw his head into his hands.

He looked a mess. She'd never seen him this rattled, though he had good reason to be.

"But that's not all. I called his mother. She said she was with her boyfriend and she'd left Mikey plenty to eat. Then she said, 'My boyfriend gave me a gold necklace. Real gold. Do you give your girlfriend real gold?' I told her, 'No, ma'am, I haven't given my wife any gold in the past couple weeks.'

"She said she'd be at the school to get Mikey." Jason looked at his wife. "I waited until eight o'clock. All the staff had left. The paramedics had checked Mikey, given him some fluids, and cleared him. I ordered him a meal and waited with him in the principal's office."

Mila couldn't speak a word. She couldn't defend the parent, who engaged in horrific negligence. She felt for the child, who didn't deserve to be parented by such an unfit mother.

Jason turned to face Mila again. "But she never came. I'd had enough and called the Child and Family Services. They sent a social worker who arrived two hours later."

"What'll happen to him?"

"Well, he'll go to a shelter. Then the Department of Children and Family Services will decide what to do next. Maybe send him into foster care."

"I hope so. What a terrible ordeal he had to endure."

"Yeah, if he goes back to his mother, she'll starve him all over again."

Jason leaned back against the sofa, his back sinking into the soft cushions. He seemed to finally relax after a calamity that had clearly shaken him—one that shouldn't have occurred in any day and age. In some places, trials and tribulations like this never happened. Mila knew of just such a place. But she didn't bring it up during her husband's moment of anguish at the unnecessary hardship of a child.

His gaze fell to the floor. "I don't know why people have kids when they don't want to take care of them."

Mila ran her hand over her husband's shoulder and tilted her head to the side, her glossy brunette hair falling in strands, straight as lines of geometry, over her cheek.

Chapter 3

Mila didn't broach the topic of moving to Coolbeensia during the next three days. Her husband took time to agree on big decisions, and relocating to an independent nation was a major life upheaval that required careful contemplation. Nevertheless, she knew when she was right. She just had to be patient.

Friday morning arrived, and Mila gobbled up her breakfast, a strawberry-and-cream-cheese pastry. Jason took a bite of burnt toast and a long sip of black coffee. They met at the front door and gave each other a quick kiss before heading off in opposite directions to their respective schools, Mila to Zebrada Elementary and Jason to Wolverstein Elementary.

Mila's fourth graders called her Mrs. Winston. She quite enjoyed hearing it, as it had a nice ring, given she'd taken her husband's last name upon their marriage.

She administered the online test on the various nouns and pronouns and let the kids tackle the morning challenge. As they kept their heads down, scrutinizing the descriptive words of people, places, things, and ideas on their tablets, she prepared a noun lesson plan, a noun list, and a fun-but-educational speech game they'd play later that afternoon.

The school day progressed swimmingly until the midday lunch hour. Mila walked into the teacher's lounge, said hello to her fellow teachers, and pulled out her bowl of cheesy pasta from the fridge. She warmed up her lunch and sat down at the long table seated with nine other teachers.

The women discussed the latest fads in hairstyles, as if they determined the final fate of the world.

"Curtain bangs are too glamorous for daytime," Susan argued, chomping on her egg salad sandwich in between bursts of vitriol against the lack of panache in contemporary hairstyles.

Fluffing her own blond bob, Geniene added, "Asymmetric bobs are all the rage."

"Oh, even better is the blunt bob," Amanda pointed out, leaning in to voice her opinion, as if it was highly classified information. "So futuristic and stylish. You never hear those two words in one sentence."

Mila listened to their senseless chatter and sighed. She swirled the cheesy Alfredo pasta around the bottom of the plastic bowl with the tines of her plastic fork. Debating hairstyles failed to excite her.

Out of nowhere, Natalia ran into the lounge, huffing and puffing. Her face flushed and her eyes wide as dinner plates, the teacher set her hands on the lunch table and exclaimed, "Ladies, Wolverstein Elementary is on lockdown. Someone brought a gun to school!"

Mila shot a look at her. "That's where my husband works!"

She dove for her phone in her back pocket, her fingers texting as fast as bolts of lightning. Her skin reddened, and her throat grew constricted. She no longer had interest in her pasta bowl, which sat untouched.

An unendurably long fifteen seconds later, she received her husband's text. Mila placed her hand on her chest and exhaled. She closed her eyes and let her head fall back over the chair.

"Is he all right?" Geniene asked.

Mila nodded. Struggling to speak after the near shock of her life, she managed to reply, "He said everything's under control. They're all safe."

She let the relief sink in as the rest of the afternoon slowed, like a stray cloud refusing to budge in a darkening sky. The clock forgot to tick. She kept glancing at it, but the hands seemed to remain frozen in the same place. Mila's attention wavered from her intended lesson plan.

"Mrs. Winston, what're you looking at out the window?" Astair asked, pushing up the glasses that were too big for his freckled face.

Mila shook herself. "Oh, nothing, just the birds are so pretty today."

"I don't see any birds," Astair said.

Her students were observant, a little too observant during this time of uncertainty. Mila twisted her nose and cleared her throat. "Kids, why don't you read silently for the next hour. Your choice of story," she announced to the class.

Her fourth graders cheered and brought out their tablets and opened their favorite books.

Mila tapped her fingernails on her desk amid the unbearable silence. A keychain fell out of one of her student's pockets, and her attention snapped toward the clanking sound. Not knowing what was happening at Wolverstein Elementary kept her on edge.

At long last, three o'clock came, and the children laughed and hollered as they grabbed their backpacks and shuffled out of the door to the awaiting school bus.

Mila supervised her students until every last one of them hopped onto the bus.

Then she got into her car and drove. It was the longest drive home she'd experienced, even though she lived only five miles away from the school. She pressed the brake at an octagonal stop sign and watched the crossing guard, dressed in yellow, help a kindergartener cross the street. Why would a crossing guard wear cheery yellow on a horrible day like this?

Disregarding the joys experienced by the rest of her world, Mila turned into the quiet cul-de-sac of her suburban home. Once inside, she couldn't bring herself to prepare dinner, much less eat—at least not until she heard from Jason.

Her husband didn't show up at five o'clock, when he usually returned from work. Mila paced the floors, her brows knitted and her face pale as a ghost. The blood had fled from her face the moment Natalia reported the gun incident at her husband's school, and it had yet to return. Even though Jason had texted her everyone was safe, things could've shifted in an instant. She knew better than to text him again out of worry, as such a dire predicament demanded the full attention of all the reasonable adults there.

Six thirty arrived, along with the sound of Jason's car engine in the driveway. Mila raced to the front door and swung it open. She stood at the doorway, biting her nails until Jason plodded up the walkway.

"You heard?" Jason slung his jacket over his shoulder.

"I heard. What happened?" Mila asked, rushing toward her husband and yanking him inside by the arm. This was the second time in a week that a serious incident had occurred at the same school.

"Everyone's okay." He swung his jacket and dropped it onto the couch, onto which he also dropped.

Mila plonked down next to him. She quietly pulled at her long hair as he began to explain.

"It was Billy, Raymond's student. Apparently, in the boy's bathroom, Billy had showed off a gun to one of my students, Chris. He'd brought it to school in his backpack."

"That's terrible." Mila's brows drew together.

"Yeah. Lot of things could've gone wrong. Chris reported the incident to me, and I informed the principal. We confiscated the gun from Billy and had him sit in the principal's office until his parents arrived."

"How'd he get the gun?" Mila asked, her knee bouncing.

"Billy said his father kept guns lying all over the house. No locked cabinets, no safeguards. They just lay there out in the open."

"How irresponsible, especially with a nine-year-old in the house," Mila said with grave concern.

Jason sighed long. "His father finally stopped at the school. You wouldn't believe what he said."

He looked at his wife with wide eyes. "I informed him his son brought a gun to school and put others in danger. Billy's father replied, with all seriousness, 'Gimme a break. What's he gonna do? He's nine!'

"I told him, 'Exactly, sir. He's nine. A child's brain doesn't mature until at least twenty-one, more likely twenty-five. And some,' I said looking him straight in the eye, 'don't mature until well past forty-five. You ought to have kept the guns locked in a safe.'

"I nearly lost my temper and wanted to scream at him that he's an irresponsible parent who put the whole community at risk. I was about to lose it when, Ed, the principal, warned the boy's father that if it happened again, Billy would be expelled."

Jason rubbed his forehead. His gaze flitted around the room, never settling on an object.

Mila sat too stunned to utter a word.

"It's no use, though, to expel a child when a serious incident like this occurs, especially when the conditions that created this potential disaster stay the same," Jason said.

"You mean the parents?" Mila asked.

"Yes. If nothing changes, then Billy will be expelled. Our school will be safe, but without parental intervention, he'll just do the same thing at another school, then another."

Jason paused and looked up at the ceiling. Sweat saturated the skin on his forehead and dripped down his temples. His light-blue dress shirt showed dark spots under the arms.

He dropped his chin. "I don't know what I would do if we had kids one day and this sort of thing happened."

He rubbed his eyes. "But—"

"Yes, dear?"

"There's one place, based on what you're saying, where there's a very slim chance, almost nil, of this kind of thing happening—where parents are über-responsible and keep their kids and others safe."

Mila's eyes sparkled, and the beginnings of a smile appeared. She sat up, alert. Pressing her lips together and sitting still as a statue, she listened intently to her husband's next words.

Jason turned and grabbed Mila's limp arms. "Honey, we're moving to Coolbeensia!"

"Hurrah!" Mila shouted, throwing her arms up. "We're moving to Coolbeensia!"

She gave her husband a big smooch on the cheek. "I knew you'd come around."

She waltzed out of the living room and all the way into the bedroom. She hummed a tune as she performed her nighttime routine. Just before bed, she did a little jig on the spot, then sank under her downy covers, sleeping soundly for the first time in days.

Chapter 4

"When are we moving, dear?" she asked on Saturday morning, as she poured freshly blended homemade batter into the hot fancy waffle maker Jason had gifted her for her twenty-seventh birthday. It had the square grids so she could prepare decadent Belgian waffles. Starting the day with her favorite breakfast was due after hearing the life-changing good news.

Her husband hunkered down at the kitchen table, his nose lifting to inhale the scent of waffles wafting through the room. "Huh? Oh, well, we should finish out the school year."

A drumming sounded in Mila's chest. "So, June first?"

"We're out too. Sounds like a plan."

She pressed down the top of the waffle maker. It sizzled. She let the batter cook for five minutes. With a spatula, she popped the fresh square waffles out of the cooking plates and stacked them onto a large blue serving dish. She sat down with Jason for a breakfast of waffles drizzled with maple syrup.

Jason scrolled on his phone. "We ought to put the house up for sale, since we're moving in less than two months."

Mila took a bite of her piping hot waffles, doused in thick, sweet syrup, the gooey kind that made it hard to say a mouthful. "Mm-hmm. Geniene knows a realtor who can get it on the market, like tomorrow. She has a track record of selling fast too. I'll call her this afternoon."

Within days, their house was on sale, ready to be moved in after June first.

The next month and a half sped by, but not without kids running away to escape barbaric parents or because they felt unwanted.

Mila and Jason packed up their possessions into large boxes they'd scrounged from grocery stores, plastic crates, and heavy-duty bags they could reuse later. They donated their brown couch, kitchen table, and the rest of the household furniture. Mila gave the giant plush teddy bear to her school. Furnishings could be purchased at their new place in Coolbeensia, once they found a suitable one.

On the last day of May, Mila wished her students a fun-filled summer. "And don't forget to be happy!" she said with a smile on her face. She'd miss those kids. They were good students. But she hoped to find another teaching job in Coolbeensia that was equally fulfilling.

She watched her beloved students climb onto the yellow school bus and wiped away a tiny tear forming in the corner of her eye. As the bus started its engine and pulled away, she waved at the children, bouncing on their seats with goofy grins splashed across their faces.

Mila pushed her shoulders back. She'd handed in her resignation earlier that day. She glanced at the one-story brown-brick school building one last time. It held fond memories, including her first day of teaching right out of college. It had been an uneventful but satisfying five years. She'd enjoyed special bonds with those kids and served as an influential parental figure for all those seven-hour days.

Then she raced home.

Jason was loading the car with jumper cables, blankets, and a first-aid kit. He returned inside and emerged with a six-pack of water bottles.

"Hon, don't forget the paperwork," he shouted as he stuffed the water bottles in the back seat of his sedan.

"I'm on it," Mila yelled back. She walked into the house and up the stairs to the bedroom. The night before, she'd packed up her and her husband's documents: passports, birth certificates and insurance papers. She grabbed the satchel where these essentials were kept and placed it near the front door so she'd remember to grab it when they said goodbye to Peoria.

Saturday morning couldn't have arrived soon enough. Mila awoke earlier than usual, at six o'clock, and stretched in her pink silk pajamas. Jason still snored next to her. He deserved to sleep in. After all, they had a long trip ahead of them.

She ran downstairs and began assembling sandwiches for their eight-hundred-mile drive to Coolbeensia. It'd take twelve hours, so she prepared enough snacks, meals, and drinks to last them on their journey. She opted for sandwiches that Jason could eat while driving. She layered smoked gouda, lettuce, and turkey slices in between sandwich rolls and slathered mayonnaise on the inside faces of the bread.

Mila arranged the sandwiches, juice bottles, and four pears into a cooler filled with ice packs. She brought it, along with the leather satchel of important documents, to the car. Standing in the driveway with her hands on her hips, she said to herself, "Food, check. Documents, check."

Jason emerged at the doorstep in his loosely untied blue robe as she loaded the vehicle. He carried a mug of steaming coffee in one hand and grazed through his uncombed dirty-blond hair with the other.

"Mornin', hon!"

"Good morning, dear," Mila said. He looked scruffy. But he'd be handsome again after a shave.

Jason looked at his watch that he hadn't taken off. "Almost go time!"

Mila smiled back.

Earlier, she'd arranged for a local kid's charity to pick up her fifteen-year-old car. She'd bought it used and knew it wouldn't survive their journey anyway.

Within a couple of hours, the husband-and-wife duo finished packing their vehicle. Mila double-checked the home, ensuring it was empty. She gave Jason a thumbs up.

Not missing a minute more, they headed off to the promise of a better life for themselves and their future family.

Mila and Jason took I-55 South until they reached Springfield, then I-72 West, headed for Jacksonville. Within a few hours, they crossed the Illinois border and entered Missouri. Kansas City was a jungle, and Jason navigated the car at a much slower pace to avoid getting lost amid the convoluted mess of highways in the densely populated city of two million.

As they drove farther southwest, Jason turned down the car stereo that had been playing staticky contemporary pop. It was the only genre of music the radio picked up that deep in the rural areas.

"You know, hon, I was thinking." The silent hum of the vehicle cruising down the highway reverberated throughout the interior.

"What's that?" Mila asked from the front seat as she eyed the lush green pastures on their scenic route.

Herds of spotted black-and-white cows leisurely munched on the wild, twisted grass, growing as high as their knees. Worn red barns, old as the days of America's adventurous pioneers, littered the landscape. Silver silos rose into the sky, towering next to the structures. It was rural pride at its finest.

"I no longer have a problem with Coolbeensian parents needing a license to have children."

"I'm listening."

"Well, I see it like this." He activated the car's cruise control as they sped down the highway at 70 miles per hour. He took his foot off the gas. "Not all parents are bad parents. There are plenty of good parents."

"Yup," Mila agreed, as she reached for a pear from the cooler. "I know lots of good parents. Some of my fourth graders have good parents." She bit into the ripe fruit. "Candace's mother is proactive in her daughter's education, showing up at every parent-teacher conference. The mutual respect between them simply awes me. She can't afford a tutor, but she always asks me how she can support her daughter, who struggles with homework. Whenever Candace aces a test, I give her a gold star. At the same time, I secretly want to give her mother a gold star too."

The greenness of the open fields sped past them, appearing almost as a blur.

"Yeah, but parents still need a license, just like all drivers need a driver's license, whether they're good drivers or bad drivers."

Mila nodded, the pear juice trickling down her chin. She leaned to grab a napkin and wiped it away.

"It's a precautionary measure that shows a person is willing to play by the rules for everyone's benefit and protection." Jason kept his eye on the long stretch of highway.

"Right," Mila said. "Earning a driver's license shows a driver knows the laws. They know how to operate a car safely and don't risk being a danger to other drivers or pedestrians."

With one hand resting on the steering wheel, Jason chimed in. "A licensed parent is aware of their responsibilities. By earning a license, they show they want the job. It proves they know how to bring up a child without jeopardizing their well-being or those of others.

"The roads would be chaos if no one had a driver's license." He shook his head. "When parents don't have a license, every day would be kinda like Wolverstein Elementary back in April."

Jason reflected out loud. "Granted, a driver's license doesn't eliminate all illegal maneuvers or accidents, but it certainly reduces them."

"And holding a parenthood license doesn't stop all perils, but it does lessen them." Mila shook her head. "In any case, I wouldn't want an unlicensed driver on the road with me."

"And I'd rather not have an unlicensed parent in my community," Jason said. "I've seen what irresponsible parents are capable of."

"Either is dangerous," Mila said. "I'm glad we're on the same page." She glanced over at her husband. She knew he'd come around. After all, she made the choice to marry him, a man who knew unquestionable rights from egregious wrongs as well as understated rights from elusive wrongs.

"Coolbeensia, though a little quirky, seems to know what it's doing." Jason looked out at the highway. Cornfields sprouted in all directions except straight ahead. "When it comes to the job of parenthood, that micronation's not a free-for-all."

A lightness tingled in Mila's chest.

Chapter 5

Mila hadn't ever been to Kansas. She'd never seen so many wild sunflowers thriving in fields that dared to go on into infinity. The car sped through miles and miles of bright yellow seas of sunflower heads bobbing carefree in the breeze. Clearly, it had earned the nickname, the Sunflower State, for good reason. Where sunflowers didn't bloom, tallgrass prairies took over the landscape.

Jason remained quiet as he drove through tranquil Kansas. Mila simply admired the state's plethora of wildflowers, fertile farmland, and the occasional sightings of sparring black-tailed jackrabbits. She laid her head back against the headrest, bathing in contentment and serenity.

The wild sunflower fields seemed to go on forever, but driving through Kansas didn't. Jason sped past the Kansas state line and entered northwest Oklahoma. She read the blue board on the side of the highway: Welcome to Oklahoma. The calm and peace abandoned Mila, replaced with angst.

Instead of clear blue skies, the sky above Oklahoma turned ominous, dark as a winding, muddy river headed for deathly falls. The wind howled, and the car shifted uncontrollably in the fierce gusts of wind. Mila glanced around, holding onto her seatbelt a little tighter.

Mesas appeared to the east, and tumbleweeds rolled onto the highway out of nowhere. Red dirt surrounded Mila and Jason in every direction. The barren plains gave off an eerie vibe, like an abandoned Old West ghost town where cowboys and gunslingers held showdowns.

"Honey?" Jason's voice broke the creepy sensation pulsing through Mila's veins. "You got any more sandwiches?"

Mila leaned down and checked the cooler. "Nope. All gone. I thought I packed enough. You still hungry?"

"Yep. Could use a snack."

"What about that oasis coming up ahead? We could stop there and grab a bite."

"Yep. See it." Jason took the next exit and entered the oasis. "Look, there's a place that sells hamburgers. Mm. I could use one right now."

He swerved the car into the parking lot, right under the large brown sign with the word *Hamburgers* written across it in big, beige lettering.

Jason parked the car and hopped out. Mila unlocked her side of the car door, lingered a bit, then exited. She watched her husband hurry into the restaurant. But something kept Mila from following. She did a three-sixty scan around the parking lot. Something wasn't right. Her instincts knew it.

The Oklahoma wind blew through her dark hair, sending the strands whiplashing across her face. She waited at the car door, her lips pursed. Then her ears picked up a sound. It was no ordinary sound. Her senses heightened, she did a slow walk around the car and then across the rows of cars in the parking lot.

The noise grew louder. It came from a vehicle parked three cars away from theirs. She dashed toward the sound and peered through the window of a compact blue vehicle. Her heart raced. A wailing baby was strapped to a car seat in the back.

She wrapped her fingers around the vehicle's side door handle. It was locked.

The June temperatures rose to above 100 degrees Fahrenheit. She knew the baby would suffer a heat stroke if she didn't get her out of there soon. Mila thought quickly. She grabbed her phone and called 911. The officials could take minutes to arrive—minutes the baby didn't have.

Mila looked around for a large rock. There had to be one around somewhere to break the window open. She spotted one on the ground, ten feet away from the vehicle, in the dry field around the restaurant. As she flung her arm back, about to break the front passenger side window, she heard a man yell.

"Hey! What're you doing? That's my car!"

She turned, her arm still above her head, holding the rock. A burly man with a floppy beer belly came out of the restaurant carrying a paper bag in one hand and an extra-large soda in the other. Mila saw the grease stains, likely from the hamburgers and fries, soiling the bottom of the bag.

The man flung open his car door, throwing the food and drink inside.

Mila grabbed the baby and cradled her in her arms. "You left your baby in the car—in a heat wave!" she screamed. "She could've died!"

Just then, Jason came out of the restaurant.

"I was gone two minutes!" the man yelled back. His bushy eyebrows popped up and down his forehead.

Jason interjected as he walked toward the scene. "Sir, you were in front of me in the cashier's line. I waited a good seven minutes for the cashier to prepare your extra-large order."

"Whatever," the man sneered.

"Well, the paramedics will be here soon," Mila said.

"You called 911?" the man asked. "What for?"

"Why else? You put your baby's life at risk."

The man continued arguing with Mila and Jason when the paramedics arrived on the scene. The EMR team checked the baby, confirming the baby's body temperature had risen dangerously high. They treated the baby with fluids and cold compresses.

Mila gave the man a piece of her mind, scolding him for his careless behavior.

She and Jason got into their car. From her side-view mirror, she watched the paramedics, with scowling faces, speak to the neglectful father.

They headed back for the highway.

"I can't believe the nerve of that man. No one should leave a baby unattended even for a minute inside a hot car. In summer, during a heat wave! Where are people's brains?"

Jason replied matter-of-factly, "Some people don't get it. This is exactly why parents need parenting licenses."

Mila folded her arms across her chest and stared straight ahead. She tried to rescue a baby in danger, but it was clear the argumentative father hadn't learned his lesson. A few burgers and a soda were more important than looking after the well-being of a helpless infant. This would happen again—but not where they were headed. In the micronation where she and her husband would make their home, every parent was trained in basic parentology.

Not far from the restaurant where their dispute took place, Mila and Jason had to pass through the local community before reaching the highway that would take them straight to Coolbeensia. Mila and Jason were but an hour from their destination.

The houses along the road looked in shambles, with wooden boards, gray as lifeless metal, and broken windows with shards so sharp they could draw blood. Crumpled litter was strewn all over the pale, yellow grass on both sides of the roads. It was amazing that anything survived here. Menacing orange dust clouds hovered overhead, threatening Mila and Jason with a fierce dust storm at any second.

Out of the dreariness, a boy in ragged shorts and a red tank top two sizes too big bolted from the side of the road. Jason slammed on his brakes, sending the wheels squealing. He turned the steering wheel hastily and averted a collision. The boy peered through the car window and flipped Jason off.

Jason gasped as he sat buckled in the car.

Mila sat motionless in her seat, too shocked to say anything.

"That was a close call," he said after collecting himself a couple of minutes later.

"Too close for comfort," Mila said. "Where are these kids' parents?"

Jason started the engine, looked both ways, and slowly drove his car back on the road.

The silent eeriness of their surroundings failed to lift.

As they continued onward, Mila's phone sounded a shrill alarm, startling her for the second time within a span of five minutes. Her hands jittery, she opened the device. "It's an alert for a missing toddler. A mother went into a convenience store and left her car running with her child in the backseat. The car was stolen and the kid's missing."

Mila glanced at her husband for a reality check. They'd had too many near disasters in just a few hours. She had to be sure she wasn't caught in some inescapable nightmare.

Jason only grunted.

After traveling for a few miles, she scrolled through her phone. Mila discovered the missing child reported earlier had been located. A preteen had stolen the car and crashed it into a tree. The toddler was found in the backseat, unharmed.

"What is this awful place?" Mila asked, shuddering.

Her husband didn't respond. Ten minutes later, they passed a rickety old wooden sign, etched with the words: Thanks for Visiting Unibrowumbia.

Chapter 6

After a short while of driving, cars appeared congested on the road. Jason and Mila approached a horizontal structure spanning four car widths and divided in sections for individual vehicles. Several cars slowed to a halt ahead of them. Above the structure hung a massive green sign: Republic of Coolbeensia.

"Look, honey, we made it," Mila exclaimed upon seeing the welcome sign to the micronation. She grabbed her husband's arm and squeezed it, and then slapped her cheek with her other palm. Twelve hours of nonstop driving, four sandwiches, and a turmoil-filled pit stop later, they'd finally arrived.

Jason leaned his head back on the headrest and exhaled. He rolled down his window and dug into his back pocket.

He retrieved his passport and set it on the console. He pulled up to the border checkpoint.

An elderly man with a nearly toothless grin stood inside a booth ahead as Jason pulled up. The border services officer asked to see Jason's and Mila's passports.

"Good day to you too," Jason said as he handed the officer his passport.

The old man flipped to an empty page, stamped it, and returned the passport.

Mila leaned across Jason and handed the officer hers. It, too, received a stamp.

As they drove off, the border officer yelled to them, "Welcome to Coolbeensia."

"We need to get a blue card to become citizens," Mila said, tucking her passport away into the satchel.

"Right. I'm headed for the immigration office," he replied, turning onto a small, dusty road. He looked to his left at the wide-open road and then to his right, also a wide-open road, and scratched his head.

Mila put their destination into her phone's GPS. It started to speak directions.

"Oh, thanks, hon." Jason followed them and soon turned into the parking lot of the Coolbeensian Citizenship and Immigrant Services building.

"Wow, I can't believe we made it this far," Mila cried out, leaning her head back and closing her eyes.

"Yeah, just one more step and we'll be Coolbeensian citizens," Jason said with equal fervor as he parked.

The couple walked toward the small building about the size of a double-door residential garage. Outside it stood a mighty silver-tone flag pole with the micronation's blue flag fluttering in the breeze.

"What a flag," Mila said, pointing upward with one hand shielding the tops of her eyes from the early afternoon sun.

"Yeah, with a smiling brown bean right in the center of it." He shook his head, chuckling. "Unheard of."

The bright blue sky made it a fine day to shed their past lives, impacted by sheer unpredictability and irresponsibility, and start afresh here in Coolbeensia— where such undesirable characteristics didn't exist. She was sure she'd be in the midst of responsible, knowledgeable parents and an entire nation that supported these excellent human qualities.

Before Mila pulled open the wooden door, she spent a few seconds admiring the Republic of Coolbeensia emblem printed on a white sheet of paper and taped to the door with masking tape.

"There are a lot more people here than I expected," Mila said as she and Jason entered. It wasn't entirely surprising, though, as the tiny ad for Coolbeensia that she'd seen in the woman's magazine must've attracted other seekers of the good life too.

They glanced around the tiny room furnished with several plastic black chairs and a lot of potted ferns.

All the way in the back was a small office with one woman surrounded by piles and piles of paperwork. In fact, she appeared so engulfed by the stacks that Mila almost didn't realize the office was staffed.

Mila walked up to the woman. "Ahem. Excuse me, but we're here to apply for citizenship."

The woman stopped handling the files and turned. She dropped her pointy chin and stared at Mila over the rim of her leopard-printed cat-eye bifocals. "Isn't everyone?"

Mila took a step forward. "This is my husband, Jason. And I'm Mila. We're the Winstons, from Peoria, Illinois. We've got all the paperwork: the passports, the birth certificates, right here." Mila brought out the leather satchel tucked under her arm.

"Have a seat," the immigration officer said.

Jason and Mila wiggled into the two chairs across from the desk.

"Tell me about yourselves."

"Well, my husband and I are elementary school teachers. We're hoping to find teaching positions here too," Mila said.

"Why do you want to become citizens?"

Jason leaned forward. "We've heard the quality of life here is amazing, especially for children." He glanced over at his wife and took her hand. "We're hoping to one day be parents ourselves. And Coolbeensia sounds like the perfect place to raise a family."

The immigration official tilted her head. She pointed toward a small black device and instructed them, one at a time, to place their index finger on it. She scanned their fingerprints and then asked them to stand in front of a camera.

"Smile for your blue card," she said, snapping a photo of Mila's smiling face, then Jason's.

"Give me an hour, with maybe an additional half, and your blue cards will be ready," the officer said. "Once you get you get your blue cards, you will be allowed to become Coolbeensian citizens after one month." She dropped her head into her piles of paperwork and disappeared behind them.

Mila and Jason got up and exited the office. "That wasn't so bad, right?" Mila said, surprised at the ease of the immigration process. "Coolbeensia sure is welcoming." They sat on the plastic chairs.

Two seats down, another couple also waited. The woman, who looked about twenty-nine, kept staring at the round clock on the wall, then checking the time on her watch. She had straight black hair, shiny as if it'd just been washed with egg whites. Mila thought to ask her about her hair routine but sat mum.

The woman leaned over and extended her hand. "Hi, I'm Vera Maybena, and this is my husband, Tim."

Mila gently shook her outstretched palm. "And I'm Mila Winston. It's nice to meet you."

Jason introduced himself. "I'm Jason Winston. We're new to Coolbeensia. You too?"

"Yep, we're from California," Tim said. "What do you do?"

"My wife and I are teachers."

"Ah, what a noble profession. I sell cars," Tim said dryly. "Used cars."

"And I used to work in a boutique. I hear there aren't too many around here, but I can sell anything anywhere," Vera said.

The two couples began chatting about life in California and Illinois, the weather, and the traffic.

Shortly after their introductions, another couple walked past, bickering.

"I did put enough gas in the car," the man said, seeming to defend himself. He trailed behind the woman, while clumsily hauling three large suitcases. He wore a neon-green sun hat and a floral Hawaiian shirt.

"We wouldn't have had to walk all the way here and leave the car on the side of the road if you had," screamed the woman, huffing and puffing and drenched in sweat. She returned the fallen strap of her above-the-knee black summer dress over her bare, bronze, sunburned shoulder.

They plopped on a seat down from Mila.

Mila turned to the woman. "I couldn't help but overhear you ran out of gas. My husband has an empty gasoline container if you'd like to use it."

Her flummoxed expression calmed. "Oh, thank you. We might take you up on your offer after we get our blue cards." She sat back, then turned again to Mila. "By the way, I'm Kaya Nowa. This is my, um, boyfriend, Simon Separa."

Simon reached his arm over and shook Mila's hand, then Jason's.

All three couples conversed over the next hour.

The immigration officer walked up and handed the six applicants their blue cards, which started the process of becoming naturalized Coolbeensian citizens. In the meantime, they were granted lawful permanent stay.

Mila looked at her brand-new blue card, which had a nice, light blue tinge to it. Across the top, it read, Republic of Coolbeensia Permanent Resident. Her black-and-white photo appeared at the bottom left corner. To the right of the information about her date of birth, gender, and country of birth was the semi-transparent image of a bright-eyed jumping bean.

She giggled from the euphoria.

After they examined their new identification cards, Mila and Jason exchanged phone numbers with Vera, Tim, Kaya, and Simon.

Vera said to Mila, "Oh, by the way, the president of Coolbeensia is holding a celebration for all new

Coolbeensians on the weekend at the presidential mansion. You should go. Tim and I will be there."

Mila thanked her for the information and said she and her husband would think about it.

Chapter 7

"A party with the president of Coolbeensia! What could be more exciting?" Mila exclaimed once she and Jason got back in their car. "And we're invited. We've got to attend."

Her husband simply smiled and drove.

"What should I wear? I brought along my best summer dresses," Mila thought out loud. "Maybe my frilly purple one." She brought her fingers to her lips. "Oh, it's regal and all but—"

"The more important question is where are we going to stay?" Jason interrupted, turning out of the parking lot.

Mila shuffled through her purse pockets and pulled out two glossy brochures. "Hon, it's all sorted. The immigration officer handed these to me on our way out. She said all new Coolbeensian residents stay here until they get settled and find jobs." She shoved the brochure in Jason's face. "Look."

He glanced down then returned his gaze to the road. "Pick a place."

"Um, okay." Mila eyed a colorful structure of cubes, spheres, and tubes pictured on the front of the brochure. Looking like it was put together from children's blue, red, and yellow playing blocks, the apartment building stood out. "We'll stay here. It's small, fun, cozy. Just right until we settle down, find our teaching jobs, and start our family. Then we'll move into a single-family home." Again, she pushed the photo in his face.

Jason pushed it away. "Just set the GPS, hon."

After she did so, she called the phone number on the brochure and spoke to the landlord.

"All set," Mila exclaimed, ending the call. "A fully furnished one-bedroom is ready for us and waiting."

"Sweet."

"Oh! We've got to stop at the currency exchange first. Coolbeensia has its own currency."

"Really?"

"Yep. They use Coolbeensian brincadors instead of US dollars."

Jason's eyebrows arched as he let out a laugh. "As in 'jumping'?"

"Guess so."

The navigational system directed them to the nearest currency exchange, where they exchanged their dollars for brincadors. Then they proceeded to their new apartment.

Everything was moving so fast, but in the right direction. Coolbeensia seemed like Bellevue or East Peoria, not much different than what she was used to. In fact, it wasn't like moving to a new country at all, but just down the street. But she'd just arrived. Every place was unfamiliar until the residents became acquainted with the laws that made or broke it.

Mila got out of the car and stretched her arms wide. She bent to touch her toes, giving her hamstrings an easeful stretch. She held onto the brochure and walked into the landlord's office. Jason waited outside, leaning against the car with his arms folded across his chest.

She came out smiling, waving a set of keys. "We're on the third floor."

"Great. Let's get unpacked."

The rest of the afternoon, Jason and Mila unloaded their belongings into their brand-new apartment. It had all they could ask for: a small kitchen with a nook for a round dining table, a bedroom snug enough for two, and a decent-sized living room.

Mila perused the brochure again for listings of nearby eateries. She phoned in an order for takeout from a Chinese restaurant boasting a handful of good reviews. Within minutes, their dinner of spring rolls, ma po tofu, egg fried rice, dumplings, and fortune cookies had arrived. She tipped the delivery guy a few brincadors and brought the steaming food inside.

The weekend nearly upon them, Mila and Jason rummaged through their open suitcases, hunting for the right dress and suit to wear to the presidential mansion.

Mila held up a yellow, floral maxi summer dress, the kind she would've worn to her students' graduation ceremony. "This is perfect. Summery, formal enough for a meet-and-greet with the esteemed president of a fine micronation." She held up the dress against her petite body and swayed. "What do you think?"

"It works." Jason got ready in his black slacks, white jacket, and a striped black-and-white shirt he'd ironed an hour before. He pulled at his black silk handkerchief, popping out of his front pocket. "There."

"Ready?" Mila asked at the front door. Jason held his arm out, and she took it.

"I can't believe we've been invited to meet the president." Mila chatted nonstop during their car ride. "I wonder how the mansion will look. I bet it's got an Olympic-size swimming pool, with water as clear and blue as the sky, a manicured lawn bigger than a football field, and an attentive butler, or two or five, who cater to the president's every whim."

She turned and touched her husband's arm. "Oh, and I can't image the mansion's architectural style. Maybe Georgian or Greek Revival." Her eyes popped, and she fanned herself. "Ooh, Greek Revival, with gigantic, white columns and a balcony on top where we'll peer at the rest of the nation below. We'll be like guests of an ancient Greek oligarch. Ah, I can't wait to party amid all the luxury and splendor."

"Yep, nothing two teachers' salaries could ever afford," Jason said matter-of-factly.

Within fifteen minutes, they'd arrived at their destination.

Jason squinted and tugged at his ear. "You sure the GPS is right?"

Mila checked her phone. "It says so right here: 4902 West Magnolia Street." She looked up with a blank expression. "That's where we are."

Five acres of barren land, with one spindly tree in the front yard, surrounded them. The neighbor's house appeared as a speck from where they stood.

"Well, maybe it's just the butler's place." He got out of the car.

Mila followed, biting her lower lip.

They walked up a long gravel driveway to a ranch house with a wooden porch. She grabbed her husband's arm as they climbed the cracked steps. "This is the presidential mansion?" Mila said, surveying the dry landscape around her.

She looked down at the worn planks near the front door. A natural coir fiber mat featuring a pineapple above the curvy lettering welcomed them. Mila wasn't sure if she should scrape her kitten heels on it and release the bits of gravel stuck to the bottom of her soles.

"My guess is as good as yours." Jason knocked on the door.

A balding man, with soft curls of brown hair still growing at the sides, opened the door. Unleashing a big grin, he said, "Well, well, you must be among the new Coolbeensians. Welcome!" He ushered them inside. "The celebration is just getting started."

Jason and Mila thanked him and introduced themselves. Upon walking inside, Jason asked, "You must be the butler. We're here to meet the president."

"Well, you're lookin' at him," answered the man, who, based on his paunch and unhurried mannerism, appeared about sixty.

Jason and Mila turned to each other and momentarily froze.

"You're His Excellency, the President of Coolbeensia?" Mila asked, her mouth falling open.

"Of course, who else would I be? Officially, I'm Eloney Ben Resz. But everyone calls me Eloney."

"You mean, President Eloney?" Jason asked.

"Nah, nah. Eloney's fine. My wife calls me 'El.' But it's a little too feminine for me. So Eloney will do."

He guided them inside. "Make yourselves at home. The other lucky new residents are in the back, drinking up the fruit punch like there's no tomorrow. Get it while there's still some left."

Mila fell into her husband's shoulder, and they both giggled.

She eyed the rustic décor as she walked through the hall. The walls exuded a stunning chocolate-brown color with richly hued brown drapes hanging over the large windows that let in the sunlight. Her neck tipping back, she looked up to see a chandelier made of several tiers of antlers. She stared at the impressive light fixture, the likes of which she'd never seen before. She was in for a lot of unique extravaganzas here in Coolbeensia. The present wonderments being only the start.

A large mahogany armoire stood like a mighty giant against the back wall of the living room. On its shelves lay thick books and bronze statues, probably from exotic destinations. Perhaps the president traveled overseas and brought home expensive souvenirs. Ah, a well-traveled leader. Someone like him was fit to shape the future of an entire micronation.

She stepped on an animal fur sprawled out on the floor, like it'd been alive centuries ago. The light brown rug felt furry under the soles of her shoes. She couldn't tell which animal it belonged to. Maybe a bear? Did bears live in Coolbeensia? She shuddered. Surely, the president went hunting on a safari and brought it back. She let her imagination run wild as she admired the rest of the décor.

Above the fireplace hung a large painting of a farmhouse with a group of people and a blue flag in front. The rest of the president's home appeared typical, with spotted ottomans tucked underneath a wooden desk with a couple antique lamps on top, a reclining armchair, and two light-green sofas, probably from the seventies.

Jason led Mila out the back to the deck. Nearly a dozen guests chatted at long picnic tables set up on the grass. String lights hung above them, delivering a warm glow. A bouquet of colorful balloons was tied to the edge of the refreshment table.

The heartfelt ambiance felt like home.

Drink in hand, Vera approached her. "Mila, so glad you and Jason could make it. The president is scheduled to make a welcome speech. We don't want to miss it!"

Chapter 8

Mila gathered the flaps of her dress, sat down at the picnic table, and wiggled into a comfortable position on the weather-worn wooden seat. Jason hopped onto the seat next to her, along with Vera and Tim. Kaya and Simon gave them friendly waves from the opposite end of the table.

A woman with untrimmed, frizzy, straw-colored hair, walked up to the front of the tables. She wore wrinkled khaki pants and a white T-shirt with the words *jumping beans* splashed across the top in graffiti-style blue letters outlined in yellow. She flipped the end of her red paisley polyester scarf off her shoulder. She picked up a metal fork and tapped it against a glass tumbler. In a loud, hoarse voice, the woman spoke. "Ladies and gentlemen, revered guests, may I have your attention please."

At the sound of the high-pitched clanking, the guests quieted their chatter and turned their heads in her direction.

The woman cleared her throat. "I am Her Excellency, the First Lady of Coolbeensia. Everyone calls me Margaret though. I'd like to be the first to give you an official welcome to our respected micronation. I'm pleased to say that you are now proud Coolbeensians."

The guests acknowledged each other, all nods and growing smiles.

"With that, I'd like to introduce you, if you haven't been already, to my dear husband and the esteemed leader of our beloved nation, His Excellency, President Eloney Ben Resz."

The backyard sounded with a round of clapping.

"Thank you, thank you," President Eloney said, bumbling awkwardly, as he stepped up in an olive-green military uniform with eight medals, orders, and decorations dangling off the left lapel of his coat.

"Hot day for a coat, eh?" he jested, tugging at his collar.

Mila chuckled, along with the guests.

"But necessary for formal business."

A kind, jolly expression lay on his face. It contrasted against the autocracy his military uniform represented. His gray eyes scanned the yard full of guests.

Mila crossed and uncrossed her legs. As he began to speak again, her body grew still. She didn't want to miss a single word from her new president. His decisions impacted the life of every Coolbeensian, which she'd officially be in less than three weeks.

"Folks, all of you are welcome here. We rarely deny anyone entrance. We believe in an open-door policy, promoting the good life for everyone."

The audience cheered.

Even before they quieted down, the president continued.

"Of course, a good life can only be had when we follow good laws. Coolbeensia is a maverick in the overcrowded arena of lawmakers. But rest assured, our laws are designed for maximum benefit for every single citizen, from the youngest to the oldest and those thrilled to be somewhere in between."

The guests glanced at each other, nodding.

"Coolbeensians are the backbone of our exceptional micronation. They are the reason we particularly invest in and protect our youngest citizens, who grow to be productive members of society. Without them, Coolbeensia is nothing. Well, it'd be vacant land but not as legendary."

Everyone's attention stayed glued on their speaker.

"Many of you have crossed major rivers and endured long distances to enjoy the high quality of life we offer. People have traveled from various territories of the United States, like Pennsylvania, Illinois, and California, among other foreign destinations." He peered into the crowd with his hand over his bushy brows. "I see a few happy faces from Ireland, Myanmar, and Greece."

The Greek-Coolbeensians, the Irish-Coolbeensians, and the Burmese-Coolbeensians patted each other on the backs.

"Whatever parts you're from, you've made the right decision. Coolbeensia is unlike any other sovereign nation in the history of the world. Every individual is given priority here. Rejoice, as your lives are about to get a thousand times better."

He raised his glass of red tropical punch to the crowd. They jumped to their feet, clapping hysterically and hugging each other.

Jason and Mila also took part in the roaring standing ovation and hugs.

As the crowd settled and dug into the nachos, a warm vat of liquid cheddar cheese, and chilled pasta salad, President Eloney visited the tables, conversing with his guests like a highly important dignitary should. He was in the business of politics, after all, even though she was certain elections weren't held in Coolbeensia.

The president hadn't yet reached her table, so Mila helped herself to more nachos, munching on them upon returning to her seat.

As she entertained a mouthful of cheese, the president approached.

"Margaret is a prize-winning chef, capable of satisfying any crowd. How'd you like them nachos and cheese sauce? She swears by a five-minute recipe passed down through the generations," he gloated.

"Oh?" Mila asked, slowing her munching of the chips. "She won a prize?"

"Deservingly. I ripped off one of my own medals and handed it to her for her glorious achievement in the exquisite preparation of nachos and their accompaniment, cheese sauce as yellow as the sun." He bent down toward Mila's ear. "If you ask me, she earned every bit of that chunk of metal."

Mila couldn't help but laugh.

At once, she saw an opportunity to rub shoulders with the official holding the highest position in the entire micronation. She straightened her posture and got serious.

"So, um, President Eloney—"

"Please, just Eloney."

"Are you really Hungarian, Eloney?"

"Me? I'm from Ohio. Columbus, specifically. Christopher Columbus's namesake. My grandparents came from Hungary on a ship that landed on Ellis Island. That makes me Hungarian American Coolbeensian." He slapped his thigh and laughed. "It's ironic, eh, how Columbus discovered America, and I founded Coolbeensia."

"Hmm, interesting. How exactly was Coolbeensia founded?"

Eloney threw his head back, his military cap nearly falling off his bald head. "It's been years. I mean, Coolbeensia's founding date was July 1, 2000 CE. Long time ago! We started with a handful of passionate citizens on a few acres. Our population boomed in no time." His gray eyes turned misty. "Now, our independent nation is home to five hundred thousand dedicated Coolbeensians. And we haven't stopped growing."

"Wow," Mila said, wiping bits of gooey cheese from the corners of her mouth with the back of her hand. She and Jason were among the recent influx of citizens. "How'd you manage it all?"

"It's a family affair. We've got five kids, and they all work hard for the Office of the President."

"You must be proud. I imagine it's a big job."

"Yeah, yeah. It keeps things orderly. Ren, my eldest at twenty-five, is our minister of stand-up."

"Stand-up?" Mila asked. Surely, Coolbeensia had forward-thinking ministers who took unconventional routes to elevate the lives of citizens to crowning heights.

"Uh-huh, as in stand-up comedy. No nation would be intact without a sense of humor. Ren keeps us all in good spirits."

"How refreshing!" She'd never considered the importance of humor to a nation's well-being. But it made perfect sense. It's no wonder so many countries were always miserable and on the brink of war.

"Then there's my son, Kai, who's twenty-four. He serves as the minister of off the beaten paths."

"Quite appropriate, considering." If anything was off the beaten path, it was Coolbeensia. But she was liking being here already.

"Aiden is twenty-three and our admirable minister of ikebana."

"I adore ikebana," Mila exclaimed, slapping her rosy cheeks with her palms.

"I'll have him sign you up for some classes. Flower arrangements are a big deal here in Coolbeensia. Keeps the neighborhoods pretty."

"Oh, definitely. I used to plant annuals every year and pick the blooms. I plan to do the same here once Jason and I find a home. The harmony between flowers and the space around them is so important."

"Consider me 100 percent on board." Eloney cleared his throat and finished his introductions to his family. "Finally, my twins Stephanie and Ada, at twenty-two, are our ministers of ethnic food tours."

Mila licked her lips.

"Their job is to introduce cuisines from all over the world. Ever heard of brownies?"

She placed her hand on her chest. "I could die for a pan of chewy brownies. I make them all the time. Though, I cheat a little and use a mix. Homemade or not, they definitely hit the sweet spot."

"Well, here in Coolbeensia, we've altered the traditional recipe and bake black bean brownies. I'm proud to say it's our national dessert. I can't imagine Margaret didn't set some out today." He glanced back at the refreshment table.

"Black bean brownies. What a mouthful." Mila laughed. "Sounds healthier too."

Eloney tilted his head. "Eh, not so much. Diabetes or not, none of us could resist 'em."

"Coolbeensia seems like a perfect nation," Mila said with a sigh. "I can't wait to start a family here."

The president thrust his chest out. "We take pride in our special micronation. We've maintained peace and stability for twenty-five years. No big wars, no little battles, not even with Unibrowumbia."

"Unibrowumbia?" Mila shivered. "It sounds familiar." She paused to think, and the color drained from her face. "I remember. We passed it on our way into Coolbeensia. What a dreadful place."

"Yep, the micronation's a big contrast to Coolbeensia. They've got no laws, no enforcement of the no laws, nothing really worth bragging about."

Unibrowumbia is a micronation too. Mila dropped her head in a few seconds of contemplation.

"If a conflict did erupt, how would you protect the people of Coolbeensia? I mean, as commander in chief, and all," she said.

"I exercise supreme command over our army, navy, and air force," Eloney said, his face beaming round and bright as a full moon. "They'd be the first to call. Our naval fleet is equipped to deter aggression around our peaceful micronation. Our marine corps is ready for combat operations, and our air force has rapid air space capabilities to subdue enemies."

Standing tall, with his legs in a wide stance, he leaned down to assure her. "Don't you worry your little head. We've got what it takes to fight the bad guys."

Mila stared out blankly and crunched on a cheesy nacho.

Chapter 9

Peter pressed his lead foot on the gas of his rusty, beat-up Chevy, weaving recklessly in between cars on the highway. Racing after him, a police car blared its sirens. He'd been on car chases before. This time was no less of an adrenaline rush. His big, hairy hands held onto the steering wheel as he grimaced.

"Hurry!" Amelia cried out. She pointed. "Take that exit."

He swerved onto the ramp. His screechy tires barely hugged the road as the Chevy careened around the edge of the ramp. They exited into a small, busy town, surrounded by rows of one-story buildings and lots of traffic on the gravelly two-lane road.

Peter spied a dark alley, pulled in, and shut off the engine. He and Amelia ducked under the dashboard. The police siren sounded louder, then faded as the squad car whooshed past.

Peeking up, Peter exhaled. "Phew, the cops missed us." It was pure luck that he'd stumbled upon an empty alley in this unfamiliar town off the highway. Had it escaped his notice, he'd surely have been caught.

"All clear?" Amelia asked, keeping her head of shoulder-length hair beneath the dash.

"Yep. Coast is clear."

She inched up her heavy body from under the dashboard.

Peter's heart rate steadily returned to normal after nearly thumping out of his chest while he fled from the police. They were hot on his trail. But he had no desire to be caught and punished with jail or fines. He'd seen the insides of too many jail cells and never grew accustomed to living behind bars.

Starting the engine, he slowly pulled out of the alley. The car crawled until it reentered the highway.

"Where we headed?" Amelia asked, pushing wisps of brown-and-silver hair off her face.

"Dunno. Thinkin' west, far from Kansas," Peter said.

"Yeah, we're on the cops' radar back home. How 'bout Unibrowumbia?"

"Unibrowumbia?" Peter wrinkled his nose. He grew devoid of all emotion. "Not that dump. That's where I spent my boyhood. I honed my entrepreneurial skills there," he said, staring ahead coldly at the road.

"You mean drug-dealing skills," Amelia said.

"I prefer *entrepreneurial* skills," Peter said in a firm tone.

Amelia turned to face him. "In the five years we've been dating, you never told me you grew up in Unibrowumbia."

"Eh, it's nothin' to brag about." Unibrowumbia deserved to stay in the closet. The less anyone knew about that freaky skeleton, the better.

She folded her flabby arms across her heavy chest. "Just goes to show how much you know a person." Amelia returned her gaze out the passenger side window.

"Besides," Peter added, "we wouldn't make a dime there."

"Why not?"

"Hardly no one works. They simply ain't got the dough to pay us."

"I hear it ain't got no laws. We'd be safe from the cops." Amelia's eyes twinkled.

"It's a free-for-all, yeah. But the quality of life is terrible."

Amelia placed her hand on her right hip. "Well, then where do you suppose we go?"

"I'm thinkin' Coolbeensia."

"Humph. That proper place? We won't make a buck there either." Amelia grew red in the face.

"But it doesn't have an extradition treaty with the US."

"Huh? What does that mean?" Amelia asked, contorting her lips.

"It means, darlin', that the little micronation can't deliver us back to the States on drug charges. It ain't ever had a drug problem in its history, so it never established laws against drug trafficking. We'd be safe there."

"Oh, I see."

"I'd pick Coolbeensia over Unibrowumbia any day. As a matter of fact, we can hide out in the open among every law-abiding citizen."

"And no one would know red from green." Amelia squealed, giggling with child-like exuberance.

Peter sped down the highway. A half hour later, the sky turned dark, and rumbles sounded in the distance. Amelia glanced around, her legs shaking. "Peter, this place is giving me the creeps."

"Oh, relax. We're in Unibrowumbia."

"I thought you said we're heading for Coolbeensia," she cried out.

Peter slowed down. "I did." He parked the Chevy in front of a broken-down house, with a white-and-green sheet for a front door.

"Where are we?"

"I'll be right back." He hopped out of the car and pushed his way through the billowy sheet.

"Peter," Amelia screamed. "Don't leave me here alone!" She wrapped her arms around her trembling body, her eyes blinking rapidly as the gloomy atmosphere closed in. She jumped at every little twitch of a branch or the scurry of a jackrabbit across the deathly parched landscape.

Ten minutes later, Peter returned.

Amelia was asleep, her head on her shoulder and drool spilling out of her open mouth. She awoke when her boyfriend slammed the car door closed. "Huh?"

"Here, we'll need these." Peter handed her two cards.

"What're these?"

"They're our Coolbeensian IDs." He started the engine and drove back toward the highway. "My cousin, Fred, specializes in parody driver's licenses."

"Ooh, I couldn't tell a real from a fake." Amelia turned over the card in her plump hands. "Look here, the lamination is peeling at the edge." She squinted at the card. "And the font looks funny. Petey, why are the letters out of alignment?"

"Oh, give the guy a break. Fred recently switched his business over to fake IDs when his parodies weren't rakin' in the profits."

"I see why parody driver's licenses ain't a hit."

Peter forged onward, seeing the Coolbeensian border sign a mile ahead. "We can't go through there. Those nosy immigration officials will discover our criminal records."

"Nooo. We don't want that," Amelia said.

He drove around, looking for just the right spot.

"There, see?" He pointed to an unpatrolled section of the border. Though, none of the micronation's borders were really patrolled with any integrity. "We'll wait here until nightfall, then sneak through that opening to freedom."

Amelia nodded as her eyes closed.

Peter munched on beef jerky and three bags of corn chips until the sun went down a few hours later. Driving slowly, he steered his car silently through the opening.

"We're home free," Peter shrieked.

"Uh, huh?" Amelia awoke, still drowsy.

"Just need to find us a place now." He'd rather not spend the night in his Chevy. The last time he did, he awoke to a policeman shining a flashlight through his driver's side window. He didn't need another close run-in with the law.

Peter continued driving until he reached the town. A colorful building of cubes, spheres, and tubes, the most unique around, with lights on inside, caught his eye. He turned into its parking lot. "How 'bout that? The sign says Apartment Building. Looks just right to me." He opened the car door. "I'll be back."

Amelia didn't bat open an eye.

He returned twenty-five minutes later and jangled new keys in front of his girlfriend's face.

"Wha?"

"We're in the basement."

"A garden apartment?" Amelia asked, still groggy.

"It's the cheapest they had. I snagged it. Come on, let's go."

Peter and Amelia grabbed their snacks and sodas. They turned in for the night in their tiny, one-bedroom furnished basement apartment with a clear underground view of the sidewalk.

Chapter 10

Amelia tore open her second snack bag that morning and munched on a handful of thin, oily potato chips while gazing out at their apartment building from the driver's side of the Chevy.

Peter stared at the architectural wonder too, slowly chomping on chips.

"It looks kinda like a playground, but for adults," Amelia said. "I bet you could crawl through the tubes connecting the rooms, like on a children's playground. Or maybe spin inside the pink-and-yellow-colored rooms like on one of those teacup rides at the amusement park."

Her boyfriend sat in a daze, in complete awe. He hadn't gotten a decent look at the unique building in the darkness last night when he'd spoken to the landlord about renting a room there.

"Speaking of children, Petey, I think . . . I think I have some news," she said, crunching another greasy chip.

"Not now," Peter huffed from the passenger seat. Potato chip crumbs fell onto his striped blue-and-brown sweater vest, which showed off his big, hairy arms. He wore the vest without a shirt underneath, just how a men's knitted vest was intended to be worn. Amelia had been a thoughtful girlfriend and knitted it for him for his thirtieth birthday a few months earlier. "We've got to find out what to do."

"What *are* we gonna do?" she asked.

"We can't go back to the US. We're wanted on drug charges." He snapped open a can of warm soda and guzzled half of it down. "We'll lay low here for a while."

"But how're we gonna make ends meet?" Amelia wiped her oily fingers on her T-shirt.

"Yeah, we ain't gonna find customers here." Peter's eyes sparkled. "I know. I'll do what I did before, a few plumbing jobs here and there. Every town, state, and nation could use a plumber."

He told Amelia to start the car. "Let's drive around. Scope out the place." He let his fleshy, bare elbow hang out of the window. The crumpled, empty potato chip bags littered the car floor.

"All right." She didn't sound too confident.

Amelia revved up the engine and drove around town.

"Now, I don't know nothin' about micronations. But this Coolbeensia, it's just like back home in Kansas. It's got

72

that small-town vibe. If I didn't know no better, I'd think I was back in my small town," she said nonchalantly, while turning the steering wheel.

Peter just looked out the window, mum as a pigeon scouring for morsels.

"I mean, it's got the roads, those great big telephone poles, and red stop signs that make you want to slam the brakes. The buildings don't look too odd, except for our apartment. That thing's outlandish. Freaky wild." Her eyes popped for a second. "But everywhere else just looks like good ol' Kansas."

Her boyfriend sat quietly, gazing at the one- and two-story buildings squished together on the sides of the streets. Each building had its own special color: orange, yellow, blue, or pastel green. Trees and benches lined the sidewalks. People walked arm in arm along the sidewalks with full shopping bags.

They passed by a bar, though it was labeled *Saloon*. Parked on the grass out front stood an old-fashioned carriage—but with no horse. Then the car whizzed past a giant red sign that read, Main Street, extending vertically from the side of a building.

"Look." She pointed. "Coolbeensia even has a Main Street like every town in the US has."

His silent gaze shifted from building to building.

Amelia and Peter hadn't gone more than five miles when a police car crept up behind them silently. As soon as it was bumper to bumper, the officer turned on his siren.

"What?" Peter spun around. "Oh, crikey. I didn't even see him comin'!"

"We can't run now. He's too close." She stopped the car on the side of the road.

The officer, in a pressed blue-and-brown uniform with a brass five-star badge pinned to his shirt, walked up as Amelia rolled down her window.

He peered into the car. "Do you know how fast you were going?" he asked matter-of-factly.

"Um, no, officer," Amelia said. "Maybe forty miles per hour? It could've been forty-five or—"

Peter pinched the skin of her hip discreetly.

She turned. "Ouch! What'd you do that for?"

"Ma'am, the speed limit is thirty miles per hour. License and registration," he demanded.

Blinking rapidly, Amelia huffed and puffed and pulled out her driver's license. She handed it to the officer. "Here you go," she said with a smile.

He curled his lips as he examined the card with the lamination peeling at the corners. "Ma'am, please step out of the vehicle."

Amelia dropped her head in her hands. "What for?" she cried out in a muffled voice. "We didn't do nothin' wrong. Nothin' at all! We was just drivin' around like good folks who ain't never broke no law." Her plump face grew red and her tone hysterical. "Besides, I think I'm pregnant."

"You're pregnant?" Peter shrieked, doing a double take. A prickling sensation crawled down the back of his neck. The cops were on his radar—not a baby. "Why didn't you say so?"

She turned to her boyfriend. "I tried to tell you."

The officer gazed at them both, clearly unimpressed. "You, sir, are the expectant father?"

"Uh, I sure hope so."

"Permit or license, please," the officer demanded again.

Amelia tucked her silver-streaked hair behind her ear. "I just gave you my license," she said, growing fidgety.

Behind his aviator sunglasses, the police officer's face flushed red. He leaned into the window. "Ma'am, you gave me your driver's license. I'm asking to see your parental license or permit."

"A what? What in the world are you talkin' about?"

"Ma'am, in Coolbeensia, it's unconstitutional to have a child without a license. Expectant parents like you are legally required to hold a permit at the least. I'm going to have to write you up for a violation."

Speechless, Amelia turned to her boyfriend, who sat dumbstruck.

Peter's flight response intensified. He'd taken two knockout punches that morning: a run-in with the police that nearly exposed his questionable past and the startling revelation that his girlfriend would make him a dad soon. Mulling over the bombshell she dropped, he sat drenched in a pool of sweat gushing out of his pores like he was the Niagara Falls during peak tourist season.

The officer created a digital ticket, which he printed on a thermal printer on the spot, and handed it to Amelia. "See you in court." He walked away.

"Our first morning in Coolbeensia and already we got to show up in court," Amelia complained.

"Who'd a thought?" Peter muttered half dazed, referring to both the ticket and his unborn child.

On the day of their court hearing, Peter and Amelia arrived, he in his sleeveless sweater vest and she in her extra-extra-large lavender T-shirt. He hadn't seen the inside of a courtroom in a long time—a nice long, peaceable time—thanks to his knack for quick getaways. But today broke his winning streak.

The clerk called their case, and the couple plodded up to the front. The officer who issued the ticket gave his testimony. "Your honor, Ms. Bord and Mr. Losor each received a ticket for not carrying a permit as expectant parents are legally obligated to do." He quickly added, "I also believe they presented fake IDs."

The judge, who happened to be President Eloney Ben Resz, sat at the bench in his flowing blue robe. "Fake IDs? Where are you really from?"

"We're from good ol' Kansas," Amelia said with a proud Midwestern smile.

"Kansas, eh? Well, fake IDs aren't the main issues here. We welcome everyone who follows the rules. Do you, Ms. Bord and Mr. Losor, have any objections to the charge?"

Amelia stood frozen. "Uh, uh, no."

Peter hesitated, bewildered by the absurd law he'd never heard of before entering this curious micronation. If only he'd known what a parental license looked like, he wouldn't be in this mess. He could've had Fred print up a fake one before he and Amelia entered Coolbeensia's borders. Was it a bulletproof polycarbonate card, like a driver's license? Or more like a thin, plasticky plumber's license? Heck, it could've even looked like a paper physician's license he'd seen framed and hanging on the doc's wall when he went in for his checkups every six or eight years.

His mind whirring with possibilities, Peter felt the guilt inch up his throat. He swallowed hard.

The judge addressed him again, this time louder.

Blinking, Peter shook himself out of his spiraling self-blame and answered, "No, your honor."

At once, Judge Eloney struck his gavel. "The verdict is guilty. Ms. Bord, you and your boyfriend, Mr. Losor, are in violation of the excellent laws of Coolbeensia, which have stood the test of time and produced healthy and happy citizens—proof that our laws work. As an expectant mother and father, you have neglected to obtain the necessary permits. Therefore, you are entitled by law to due punishment."

Amelia's eyes welled up.

The judge looked into her large eyes flooded with tears. "But I have a soft spot for expectant mothers." The lines on his face softened. "You and Mr. Losor will be given a chance to earn your licenses. You will attend parental school, our very own Resz Parenthood Polytechnic." Gazing at them, he said, "Ms. Bord and Mr. Losor, you will start classes in two weeks."

He banged the gavel. "Case dismissed."

Chapter 11

Mila and Jason returned to their apartment.

"Another great day." Mila waltzed in and plopped on the couch. "I can't believe we found teaching jobs so fast."

"Mm-hmm." Jason hung up the keys on the wooden rack by the door. "Every one of my fourth graders is well-fed, doing well academically, and unbelievably happy. I've never been surrounded by unstoppable cheer. Plus, I haven't had one disastrous incident yet. I don't expect I will."

"The kids will grow up to be fine adults, contributing to Coolbeensian society like it's second nature. As our president said, citizens are the backbone of our nation, and it all starts with the kids." She looked at her nails, which had been trimmed yesterday. "It's the way they're treated here—nurtured by responsible, skilled, and willing parents—that makes Coolbeensia the coolest place to be all around."

She lay on the couch, throwing her legs up on the armrests of the chocolate-brown couch, which happened to be the same color as their first couch in their home in Peoria.

Mila checked the clock. It was too early to prepare dinner.

She sprang up. "Speaking of it, I hear the Resz Parenthood Polytechnic is rigorous. I mean, the parents of my students passed, but they all said it was no piece of cake." Her brow wrinkled.

"Not to mention the Parenthood Competency Test we have to take afterward. It's the final step before we earn our parental licenses." Jason undid a few buttons at the top of his light-blue dress shirt.

"Don't forget the oath we give at the Office of Parenthood. Then," she added with a smile, "we'll officially be licensed to practice parenthood!" She fell back on the couch, throwing her arms in the air. "I can't wait to start school and earn our licenses. We'll finally be ready to start our family the right way." She hugged the couch cushion tightly against her chest. "It's all I want."

Jason gave her a sideways glance. "Calm your horses. We haven't even begun school yet."

"We ought to prep for it. Classes start next Monday, after all." She rubbed her palms together. "If we prep now, we'll definitely be at an advantage. We have to pass. It's the whole point of moving here."

"Well, how do we prep?" Jason asked.

"One of my student's parents suggested learning how to speed read. The Parenthood Polytechnic courses involve tons of reading and analyses of real and hypothetical scenarios." Mila scurried over to her laptop on the table. She typed in the search bar. "I'll sign us up for one of these."

"What's that?"

"An online speed-reading course. It's only four hours long. We can complete it over the weekend and be all set for classes starting Monday."

"Sounds good."

"Yep. Says here that we'll learn advanced skimming techniques and how to effectively take notes." She began typing in their information in the signup section. After a few keystrokes, she exclaimed, "Done!"

Mila went to the kitchen to prepare dinner. Jason relaxed on the couch and scrolled through his phone.

Meanwhile, Amelia sat cross-legged on the low-pile carpet, manipulating two long needles and a ball of red yarn. She wrapped the yarn around her pinky finger twice, and then brought the yarn across her hands.

"I don't see why we have to go to parenting school," she grumbled, looking down at her knitting. "My mom and pop didn't go to no parenting school, and look how great I turned out."

Peter gave her a sideways glance. "Uh, right."

"High school was hard enough, and I barely passed." She looked up with her puppy-dog eyes and set her gaze on her boyfriend. "How 'bout you?"

He grunted. "High school was fun and games—except when we were in class." The corners of his lips curled up as he recalled the giant stolen beer kegs, the obnoxiously loud parties that kept the entire block up all night, and drag racing with his friends while drunk. Those were some good times.

Amelia rolled her eyes. "Now we have to be told what to do all day long." She twisted her lips. "Do this, and don't do that. Pay attention. Don't be late. Stop putting chewing gum in her hair. Humph."

She went quiet for a minute. A look of concern spread over her face. Without blinking, she asked, "Peter, have you ever thought, what if we don't pass. Then what?"

His hands in his jean pockets, he replied with a shrug of his shoulders, "I dunno. The judge never said nothin' about not passin'." He stood near the window, staring out at the knobby knees that walked by.

"I bet they'll be hard, the classes, I mean." Amelia resumed knitting.

"Eh, how hard can they be? Give the kid a bottle. Change a couple diapers every once in a while. What's the big deal?" Peter's voice escalated as his arms made jerky movements. He wasn't too enthused about going to parenting school either. He didn't need training to do the job—any job, unless it brought in the dough, and lots of it.

"Imagine that. An entire school dedicated to parenting." She set down the knitting needles on her lap and looked out vacantly. "It'll be information overload." Again, she curled her lips. "The bottle should be this temperature and not that. They have to sleep this many hours and not an hour more." She began to rapidly knit. "And don't ever forget them at the grocery store." She threw her knitting across the room. "Rules. Arrgh!"

Peter sighed. "Yep, I bet there'll be a lot of rules. I don't know how I'm gonna remember them all."

"At least the school's free," Amelia said.

"Yep. We ain't gotta go more broke than we are."

Amelia sighed. "There must be some good parts about the school to look forward to." A sly smile spread across her face. "I remember when I doubled my school lunch money."

"How'd you do that?"

"Oh, I simply told Missie Ray that if she didn't give me her lunch money, I'd yank her braids and tie 'em to the flagpole." Amelia giggled. "She told the teacher she was too sick to go to the lunchroom after that."

"Yeah, well, I don't see us making any new friends there."

"At least not *our* kind of friends. I don't see why more people ain't like us."

"It's gonna be months of pressure," Peter predicted.

"Social pressure. Academic pressure."

"Too much pressure in general."

A lightbulb went off in Peter's head. He thrust out his chest and, pointing his thumb toward himself, uttered boisterously, "No school tells me if I'm a good parent or not."

Amelia looked up. "Yeah, you're right. Who's to say? I betcha I'll be the best mom on the block. Ain't no teacher gonna tell me how to parent. If my kid comes home and tells me it got double the lunch money, I'm gonna give it the praise it deserves."

"We'll catch our kid being good," Peter said.

"And encourage their good behavior," Amelia added.

"We'll be excellent role models."

"Ain't no two doubts about that!"

Chapter 12

Mila and Jason arrived at the Resz Parenthood Polytechnic at 6:45 p.m. on the dot. It was a two-story, red-brick, pseudo-Georgian building with white columns in front and a white bell tower at the top. Mila had read earlier that it was designed by an acclaimed architect who had graduated from the school.

"I'm glad they're offering evening classes, so we can work during the day," Mila said to her husband, as they hopped up the steps to the building for orientation.

Upon locating the classroom, they waited beside a shiny antique, mahogany frame in which hung the Coolbeensia Constitution. Next to it was another aged frame encasing the Coolbeensia Bill of Rights. As they admired the documents, printed in gold lettering, other students entered.

Vera and Tim sauntered in. Vera saw Mila, waved, and rushed over.

"Mila, I didn't know you wanted to be a parent," Vera squealed, giving her a good-natured shove.

"Same here. I didn't expect to see you," Mila said.

"Coolbeensia is full of the unexpected."

As they engaged in small talk, waving their arms animatedly and laughing, Kaya and Simon strolled in. Kaya dropped her square polarized sunglasses to the tip of her nose, and scanned the room full of students. In her body-hugging red summer dress, she walked up to Mila, Jason, Vera, and Tim.

"Surprise, surprise. What're you all doing here?" Kaya asked in her nasally voice.

"For the same reason you're here," Mila said, and the group began chatting away.

As the long hand ticked seconds away from seven o'clock, Amelia and Peter plodded in, grunting, sighing, and tugging at their shirts sticking to their sweaty bodies. They plonked down at two desks at the back of the classroom.

"Told ya we'd be early," Amelia snapped at Peter. "I coulda slept in longer."

Peter rolled his eyes.

At seven o'clock sharp, the professor walked in with her nose in the air. Her chestnut hair was tied back tightly in a sleek, shiny bun. She wore a slim, gray skirt suit that hung to her knees and black kitten heels.

Mila had taken her seat. She gawked at the intimidating professor who'd provide the education that determined her future parental destiny. Mila studied her slender face and haughty expression.

"She looks world class to me," Mila whispered to her husband sitting next to her.

As Jason leaned in and began mouthing words, the professor dropped a heavy book on the podium, creating a startlingly loud boom. Mila jumped in her seat.

"Ladies and gentlemen, welcome to Resz Parenthood Polytechnic. I am your instructor, Professor Wigglebun. I'll be teaching you some of the most valuable lessons you'll ever learn in your life—lessons that will prepare you to become professional parents."

Mila followed the professor's every move, as she paced back and forth across the front of the classroom with her hands clasped behind her back, speaking through her thin, pursed lips. Mila couldn't help but notice her fine lipstick lines, which must've come from years of not smiling.

"Resz Parenthood Polytechnic is a premier educational institution with no equal. No other school in the world even remotely surpasses the dignity of and dedication to our noble mission."

Professor Wigglebun turned abruptly and faced her students.

Mila shrank back as the professor glared straight ahead.

"These next nine months will be transformative. They'll be a test of endurance unlike any you've experienced before. Under the stress, you will either thrive—or you will crumble."

Mila threw glances around the classroom, noticing a few other students also sinking into their chairs, with barely their heads visible above the desks.

"But first is orientation." The professor sat on her stool, leaving one leg dangling. "Each of you will introduce yourselves to the class." She pointed at Mila. "You may start, young lady."

Mila cleared her throat and spoke in an unusually high-pitched tone. "Uh, hi, my name is Mila Winston. I hope to become a professional parent one day, like all of you."

"And what do you do for a living, Mila?" the professor asked.

"Oh, I'm an elementary school teacher. I love my job. It's—"

"Thank you, Mila." The teacher pointed to the back. "How about you?"

Peter pointed to himself. "Who, me?"

"Yes, sir, you in the knitted sweater vest."

He shifted in his seat. "I'm Peter Losor. I'm an entrepreneur and, uh, occasional plumber."

The rest of the class gave formal introductions and then lined up in the hallway to get their headshots taken.

Upon returning to their seats, Mila raised her hand.

The professor called on her. "Yes, Mila?"

"Professor Wigglebun, what are our pictures for?"

"The photos are for my reference. I use them to call on students out of the blue." She gazed at Mila over the rim of her eyeglasses. "Don't think you can hide at the Resz Parenthood Polytechnic."

Mila, sitting very still, gulped.

The professor reached down into a cavity at the base of the podium and brought out a stack of glossy rubber-banded pamphlets. She undid the rubber band and asked Mila, who sat at the front, to take one and pass the rest to the next person.

"What're these?" Mila asked, barely getting a glance at them.

"Class, the pamphlets being handed out are a pocket-size version of the Coolbeensian Constitution. Inside the flap, you will also find the Bill of Rights. I advise you to familiarize yourselves with both. You will need them in class."

Professor Wigglebun resumed her position behind the podium.

"At the end of these nine months, you will have gained the ability to think on the spot, which will help you make the right decisions even under duress. More importantly, the grueling training will prepare you for the biggest test of your life: the Parenthood Competency Test.

Should you pass, you will earn the legal right to practice parenthood. Should you fail," she eyed the class, "accept the consequences."

The students writhed in their seats.

"When you become a professional parent, what do you hold in your hands?" She pointed to Amelia, who cringed.

"Well?

"Um," Amelia started, "dirty diapers?"

The class erupted in laughter.

Professor Wigglebun's face remained stern.

"You hold your children's futures, fortunes, and health in your hands. Young as they may be, their lives are in your hands."

She scribbled on the whiteboard. "You come to class to do three things. What are they?"

"You again, funny woman." The professor gestured toward Amelia.

"I-I don't know," she murmured almost inaudibly, shrugging.

The professor cupped her ear. "First mistake. You must speak louder." Then she addressed the entire class. "Why? Because you are learning to become professional parents, and professional parents speak with assurance."

Mila turned to see Amelia blushing.

"You are here to prepare, read, and develop your thinking skills. When you're prepared for parenthood, it's inevitable that you'll get the greatest joy out of it. It's the sole obligation of Resz Parenthood Polytechnic to prepare you for this role of a lifetime.

"Lessons are effective, provided you heed them. Preparation is more effective, as long as you make the effort. But life experience, which catches you off guard, is most effective. You'll be given hypothetical situations, and you'll learn how to apply the lessons. Class simulations are invaluable, but they're no match for real life. By the end of your hard work, you'll gain the foundations of parenthood."

Mila's eyes narrowed, noticing Peter folding his hairy arms across his chest and yawning.

"You need to learn how to think like a professional parent. If your child behaves badly and you don't discipline him, what have you done?" She pointed to the back. "Peter?"

"Um, uh . . ."

Professor Wigglebun dropped her arm. "Don't start with 'um.' It makes you sound unconfident, like you aren't sure about being here."

"Uh, well." His eyes darted left and right.

"Pause before you respond. Professional parents express confidence."

Peter sank into his seat.

She resumed her lecture. "If you fail to discipline a child upon poor behavior, *you've* done something wrong. If your child behaves well and you don't praise them, you've missed an opportunity.

"Your children will surprise you. They'll push you off balance with absurd questions, keen observations, outlandish actions. The more you know about being a parent, the saner you'll be."

Mila sat irked watching Peter distractedly pull at the tiny lint balls on his sweater. He paid more attention to his sweater vest than the teacher's lecture. He clearly wasn't taking class seriously.

"Any questions?" the professor asked.

A butter knife could've sliced the thick silence in the room.

"Okay," she said with a clap. "That's a wrap. See you in class."

The orientation ended at ten o'clock sharp. Mila exhaled. The time had sped by. She gathered her belongings and hurried out the door with the other students.

Chapter 13

"Petey, are we going to the big party?" Amelia asked one sunny Saturday morning. The skies were blue as a field of bellflowers and not a cloud drifted in sight.

"What're you talkin' about?" he asked, his voice raspy. He rolled over onto his stomach. The white sheets had tangled around his bare, hairy legs. He wasn't about to rouse himself up for a mere social event.

"You know, the Founder's Day celebration. It's today, July first." Amelia looked in the mirror as she combed her straight, chin-length hair, giving her brown-and-silver strands a neat side part.

He might as well have gotten up. Amelia had interrupted his sleeping in, and on the weekend, for goodness' sake. With gargantuan effort, he hauled himself upright and scratched his armpits.

"Eh," he said, making a shooing motion and throwing off the covers. "Nah." He smacked his lips and rubbed his stubble chin. "Founder's Day, Downder's Day." Unless someone founded him a five-story mansion complete with a garage full of sports cars, he didn't see a need to attend Founder's Day.

"Come on." Amelia pulled her boyfriend's arm. "There'll be a parade and a real-live marching band."

He brushed off her grip, as if swatting an annoying fly. "Quit pulling my arm. And how'd you know about this Founder's Day deal anyway?"

"I saw a flyer taped to the school hall." Her bubbly tone didn't make the party sound any more enticing.

"Ugh, school." He shook his head. He wasn't looking forward to going back.

"Come on, Petey. There'll be food." She leaned in, smiling inches away from his face. "Hot dogs, hamburgers. Mm." Quirking an eyebrow, she exclaimed, "And it's free."

Peter's face lit up. She'd said the magic four-letter word. "Free?" He looked at Amelia for the first time that morning. "Why didn't you say so? Come on, we're goin' to this party." He leaped out of bed.

Hordes of onlookers packed Main Street, waving miniature blue-and-brown Coolbeensia flags on the sunshiny summer day. Citizens, young and old, with their faces painted blue and brown, stood on the sidewalks, as a string marching band paraded down the street. The musicians strummed banjos, played saxophones, and banged drums to the tune of "All Bless Coolbeensia"—the national song.

Amelia, clutching Peter's arm, wove through the crowds. She and Peter found a nice spot with a view of the marching band. The sound of the musicians' singing grew louder:

All bless Coolbeensia

We love its esoterica

Our micronation is a sensation

This mighty land wins our adoration

"Oh, Petey, listen!" Amelia started mouthing the words and bobbing her head to the music.

Peter dug his hands into the pockets of his loose blue jeans and stood watching, as his girlfriend clung to him tightly. "Nice," he mustered. "I don't see the free food."

He scanned the crowds, dressed in blue-and-brown T-shirts, looking for the hotdogs and hamburgers. As he did so, his eye caught the sight of President Eloney, better known to him as Judge Eloney.

"Hey, look, the judge is here!" he exclaimed.

"Where?" Amelia squinted in the direction Peter faced. "I don't see him."

Peter pointed at the crowd on the opposite side of the street. "Over there, sitting on that lawn chair on the sidewalk. Come on."

Still holding onto him, Amelia yanked him back. "I don't wanna talk to him. He sentenced us to school."

"Gimme a break. Let's go." Peter plodded off in Eloney's direction, with Amelia stumbling behind.

He approached Eloney, who kicked back on the lawn chair, his flip-flops dangling off his feet. He looked prepared for the blazing July sun with a wide-brimmed shade hat, sunglasses, and a layer of white sunscreen down the bridge of his nose. His blue Hawaiian shirt fluttered in the light breeze.

"Hey, Judge. Never expected to see you here," Peter said as he reached Eloney's side.

Eloney glanced up. "Why not? Can't a president enjoy the birthday celebration of his own nation?"

"President." Peter's head flinched back slightly. "Where's the president?"

Eloney pointed to himself. "Right here, me the president."

"What?" Peter gave him an incredulous stare. "You're the judge. The judge who sentenced us to nine months of school," Peter cried out, his nostrils flaring.

"I'm also the president."

"Of Coolbeensia?"

"That's right. The president of Coolbeensia. But you can call me Eloney. Everybody does."

Peter's jaw dropped. His body froze.

Just as he stood flummoxed and speechless, Mila and Jason ambled up.

"Eloney! It's lovely to see you," she exclaimed. "You must be the most excited of everyone, to see all this fanfare in celebration of Coolbeensia's founding."

"Ah, yes, yes, no one's prouder than me." Eloney smiled back.

She and Jason opened up two folding chairs and positioned them on one side of Eloney. Mila gave Peter a slight nod of acknowledgment, but tightly expressed, almost disdainful.

A bit taken aback, Peter ignored Mila and took a seat on the other side of the president. Amelia stood next to her boyfriend, her eyes glued on the parade of colorful floats, giggling children, and adults dressed in flamboyant brown-and-blue outfits that showed off their patriotic spirit.

Peter's posture perked up. "If you're the judge, how can you also be the president?" he asked.

"It's my nation. I can do whatever I want. Let me put it in simple terms: I consist of not only the executive branch but the judicial branch and the legislative branch," Eloney said.

Tuning out the raucous parade, the laughter, and merriment, Peter focused on Eloney.

"As I sit on the Coolbeensian Supreme Court or traffic court or any court in between, I decide what happened and a fitting punishment, if a crime was committed, that is." He made a dismissive gesture with his hand. "But I rarely sit on the bench. Coolbeensians are typically law-abiding citizens." He glanced up at Peter. "Except for you. You're the anomaly." He returned his gaze to the parade. "In fact, people come here specifically for our laws."

Peter's posture loosened as he scratched his head.

"Then, as the legislative branch, I declare wars—but in our twenty-five-year history, I haven't had to do that once. I also sign into law bills that I introduce. Of course, I discuss any proposed bills with myself first, then I approve them. Easy peasy. In the event I veto a bill, I have the right to override it and pass it into law."

Gawking at the president, Peter didn't blink.

Just then, an ATV cruised by, pulling a utility trailer decorated with shiny blue garlands and the rare brown ones obtainable only through special order. Blue tinsel hung from the bottom edges of the trailer, almost scraping the ground. A neatly folded blue-and-brown bow with streamers accentuated the end of the trailer. Smiling school children of all ages stood inside it, waving at the onlookers.

"Are you kidding? You make all the Coolbeensian laws, like that weird one where parents need a license?" Peter asked, tottering slightly back on his feet.

"I'm not kidding. Why is it weird? It's obvious such laws are necessary." His eyes followed the trailer as it passed. "Just look at those happy kids," he said with a somewhat fatherly sigh. "It's because they were raised with utmost care by dedicated, well-intentioned parents."

A golf cart, decorated in patriotic colors, unhurriedly rode behind the ATV. Its hubcaps were covered in blue plates with pictures of brown beans in the centers. Multiple Coolbeensian flags poked out from the cart's rooftop and fluttered freely in the wind. The driver and passengers, appearing to be in their early twenties, turned, smiled, and gave friendly waves.

"See those adults?" Eloney asked, waving back.

"Yeah," Peter said, having no clue as to where this conversation was going.

"They're happy, well-adjusted, and thriving. It's because they were once Coolbeensian children."

A group of six bean mascots, in head-to-toe brown costumes, danced awkwardly to the national song behind the golf cart. The parade attendees swayed in tandem to the music, hollering with fervor.

As the parade wound down, leaving a few costumed stragglers, a young mother pulled her five-year-old in a wagon painted in patriotic colors with bouquets of blue and brown balloons floating from all four corners. The child's smile exuded unstoppable joy.

Loud pops, sizzles, and crackles sounded in the distance. Peter looked up. Fireworks shot high into the cloudless sky, mimicking rockets racing fifteen hundred feet into the air, exploding into vibrant displays of blue and brown dyes and smoke that left unpleasant sulfuric odors. He rubbed his arm, feeling the pressure waves against his skin. The sky became awash with the colors of Coolbeensia.

None of this mattered to Peter. He wasn't the patriotic sort. He looked over at Mila and Jason. They both seemed transfixed by the jubilant entertainment.

Peter spotted the food tables as the parade thinned out near the end. They were covered in shimmery blue tablecloths with a large brown sign hung in front that read, "All Bless Coolbeensia."

"Excuse me, Judge, er, President. But I'm gonna grab me some free hamburgers."

Chapter 14

Professor Wigglebun strode into the classroom at seven o'clock on the dot the following Monday. She examined the students' faces, with her brows knitted together and her thin lips tightly pursed, as if she were grading the most difficult test of the academic year and granting *F*'s across the board.

"I take it you've all had your fun at the Founder's Day celebration?" she burst out, asking the class.

Mila answered without missing a beat. "Oh, yes, Professor Wigglebun. It was the best I've ever attended. The parade and fireworks were a blast."

The professor didn't crack a smile. "Good, because that's all the fun you will have for the next nine months. Orientation is over, and class officially starts today."

The long wooden stick she used to point to various objects in the classroom ended in a sharp, pointy tip—so sharp that it might've been used effectively as a puncturing weapon against disorderly students. Mila sunk a little in her chair. Professor Wigglebun was the type who wouldn't hesitate to use it.

Clearing her throat, the professor pointed to the right side of the room. "You there, Peter, bring up that frame to the front of the class."

Peter glanced to his right. Grunting, he hauled himself out of his seat and began to do as ordered.

"No, not the Constitution, the Bill of Rights," Professor Wigglebun said. "That one."

"This one?"

"Yes, that one."

He pulled the frame off the hook and trudged to the front. He placed it on the rim of the whiteboard.

"Thank you, Peter."

She turned to the class. "The Constitution of the Republic of Coolbeensia is the supreme law of Coolbeensia. It governs every aspect of life, except when the president chooses otherwise, which is, quite often, more often than expected." She cleared her throat. "After all, he wrote it."

The professor straightened her skirt. "But what you see here is the Coolbeensian Bill of Rights. This document contains the first ten amendments to the Constitution. It guarantees freedoms to citizens."

Pointing with her long, sharp stick, she continued. "We will focus on the first six amendments, as they pertain to the purpose of your education. The other four are particular to the rest of Coolbeensian society. We won't mind about those right now."

Mila's knee bounced, this time not out of nervousness but excitement. She'd taught her fourth graders the United States Bill of Rights hundreds of times and knew the importance of being governed by sensible ones. Laws existed back in Peoria, too, but none like the progressive laws of Coolbeensia. Her new homeland's laws were the very reasons she and Jason immigrated here.

"Let's not waste another moment. We'll dive right into the first amendment." She put on her purple designer butterfly glasses, which hung around her neck on a silver chain. "Take copious notes, as you will be tested on your knowledge at the end of the term. I recommend handwritten notes as opposed to typing them, as you'll benefit from greater comprehension."

Mila brought out her notebook and pen, ready to fiercely scribble away.

"The first amendment. The most important of them. Ahem. All children shall have the birthright to willing, skilled, and responsible parents. All children shall have the right to petition the government for a redress of grievances." She turned her olive-skinned, expressionless face to the class. "In other words, Coolbeensian parents are held to high standards. If you don't want to be a parent, please choose another line of work. If you have parental aspirations, follow the profession's rules. Children may ask the government to fix problems if parents behave poorly." Peering over the rim of her eyeglasses, she said, "And as fair as President and Judge Eloney Ben Resz is, he always sides with the children."

Sweat droplets formed on Peter's temples.

"Any questions?"

The students glanced at each other wide-eyed.

"Moving on to the second amendment." She tapped the framed document with her stick again. "All children shall have the right to a safe, secure, and stable home where they have access to food, education, and medical care, plus ample opportunities to explore freely."

The second amendment seemed pretty standard. Mila tilted her head. The first amendment, though, was utterly ingenious. Back in Peoria, countless parents would've broken that law, and the government would've been flooded with grievances left and right. And rightfully so. Given the first amendment alone, she was among people who shared her ideals. She leaned forward, so as not to miss a single word.

"Under the third amendment, all children shall have the right to be respected, unconditionally loved, accepted, and guided."

Amelia shot her hand up.

"Yes, Amelia?"

"Until when?"

"Until when what?" the professor asked.

"Until what age do we have to keep respecting them?"

"Why would you want to stop respecting anyone at any age?"

"I dunno. It's just a tall ask," Amelia said, dropping her head.

"Parenting *is* a tall ask," Professor Wigglebun replied matter-of-factly. "Not everyone's cut out for it."

Amelia, her ears growing red, laid a palm on her belly and slinked into her chair.

"Okay. Let's move on. The fourth amendment stipulates that all children shall have the right to grow through opportunities for play that let their imaginations run freely."

Mila liked this one. She believed in it wholeheartedly. Back at Zebrada Elementary, she'd scheduled an extra ten minutes during the school day just for doodling, daydreaming, making slime, or painting rocks. The school administrators scolded her for wasting those few precious minutes on nonsense, but she believed wholeheartedly in the value of so-called nonsense. At last, others held a similar vision. Smiling to herself, she started to feel like she fit right in.

"The fifth amendment states that all children shall have the natural-born right to live in a make-believe world for as long as they wish, even up to adulthood. Though, Coolbeensians prefer the exceptional realities of our forward-thinking micronation to a make-believe world, any day."

Yes, they got it! Social and emotional skills developed when children engaged in make-believe play. Nothing surpassed the pricelessness of a cheap, fluffy princess dress or an orange plastic king's crown. Mila wanted to give Professor Wigglebun a big, wraparound hug for corroborating what she already knew, but she refrained in favor of keeping her excitement under control.

The professor whacked the stick on the glass of the framed document, which produced loud *tap, tap* sounds. "The sixth amendment is a popular one. I must warn you, it's asserted frequently by children, as parents oftentimes forget it. But because you are in my class, you will remember it, and I mean forever."

Except for Mila, the students squirmed in their seats.

She sat at the edge of her chair, giving the professor her rapt attention.

"Per the sixth amendment, all children shall have the right to—"

The class grew silent as an anechoic chamber, almost hearing the blinks of their eyes. It was as if every student held their breath in anticipation of a law they'd surely unwittingly break and for which they'd be penalized heavily for the rest of their lives.

"—silliness! To act silly, to speak silly, and to be all-around silly as can be."

Mila felt the tension in the class instantly release.

"And every child appreciates this inherent right all the more when their parents try, however pathetically, to be as silly."

Professor Wigglebun dropped her shoulders and exhaled. "There you have it. The first six Republic of Coolbeensia amendments most pertinent to your education and future lives as professional parents."

Setting down the stick, she shuffled papers at the podium. "You will be given assignments to enhance your comprehension of Coolbeensian law. Your first task is to memorize the Coolbeensian Bill of Rights. You should know all ten amendments like the back of your hand. Second, in preparation for next class, you will read and analyze the forty-page case *Piccadiddy vs. Piccadiddy*. Be ready for serious discussions and cold-calling. I wouldn't want to leave any of you . . . out in the cold."

The students began to gather their belongings.

"Before you run, you may have realized a good long-term memory behooves you. Everything you learn in today's class is relevant to future lessons. It provides a solid foundation for your parenting journey." Glowering over her spectacles, she snarled, "Provided you pass the competency test."

Mila shivered. She'd taken thorough notes by hand, just as the professor advised, and she intended to study them daily. She glanced around the room.

Peter hadn't even opened his notebook.

Chapter 15

Mila plopped down on the couch and patted her satiated stomach. Jason's preparation of seasoned grilled halibut and oven-roasted asparagus was remarkably satisfying, delicious, and hit the spot. Given his surprisingly exceptional skills in the kitchen, he should have dinner duty more often.

The clock struck eight o'clock. She stayed in that night to study for class. Vera and her husband were certainly out for dinner and drinks, but they had plans to spend time together over the weekend.

She opened her tablet.

Jason relaxed on the recliner with his phone in hand.

"You reading the *Piccadiddy vs. Piccadiddy* case?" she asked.

"Yep, right now," he said, scrolling through his phone.

"We're supposed to dissect the case, learn the legal principles, and see how they apply to Coolbeensian law." Her eyebrows squished together as she focused on the text. Her rigorous curriculum at the Resz Parenthood Polytechnic was nothing like breezing through undergrad. Instead, it was an intense burst of knowledge. A beautiful explosion—like a lightbulb with a snapped filament. And these crucial nine months were expected to serve her, and her future progeny, well for eighteen years at a minimum.

"Yeah, and see if it's a just outcome." Jason, too, concentrated on his screen.

Several minutes later, Mila finished reading through the facts. She turned to Jason, who still had his head in his phone.

"This is an interesting case," she said with raised eyebrows. "The younger Piccadiddy is the plaintiff, and the elder Piccadiddy, his father, is the defendant."

"I wouldn't want to be in his shoes," Jason remarked, looking up from his phone.

"Well, you won't be if you understand what the case is trying to teach us." Continuing to observe the text, she spoke in a softened voice that expressed her sheer wonderment.

"Apparently, the elder Piccadiddy immigrated from foreign shores, specifically Florida, with his young son. According to his son, he came home raging drunk one winter night, tracking in a mess of snow and ice into the house, and blurted out that Santa Claus didn't exist. The younger Piccadiddy stormed off to his room, shut the door, and unleashed a torrent of tears."

"Eh, sounds awful," Jason said, wrinkling his nose. "He was only seven."

"Hmm. Yes. The case goes on to say the younger Piccaddidy was devastated, never believing in the Tooth Fairy or leprechauns anymore either. He claimed his Fifth Amendment right, which he learned in school, was violated, causing him to be damaged for life."

"He's seven, barely getting started," Jason retorted. "And for life? Are you kidding me?"

"Well, we have to look closely at the defendant's conduct and determine if it unequivocally led to a violation of the plaintiff's Fifth Amendment rights."

"What was that right again?"

With a heavy sigh, Mila shook her head. "Jason, you should know it by now. It's Friday, and you had three days to memorize the entire Bill of Rights."

He ran his hand through his hair. "Yeah, but—"

"No excuses, Jace. We've got to prepare if we're going to be licensed parents." She put her hand on his thigh and gave it a light push. "Anyway, the Fifth Amendment states that kids have the right to live in a make-believe world for as long as they wish." She dropped her tablet onto her lap. "For sure, per Coolbeensian law, this kid's right was violated."

Jason jerked his head back. "How so? Kids at some point realize there's no Santa Claus."

"But at age seven, he had the right to be inspired by the magical world of Santa and other legendary beings. I mean, it's just plain wrong that the father's irresponsible blurt led him to no longer believe in the Tooth Fairy too. These figures add so much joy and wonder to a child's life. The father had no right to take that joy away from his son so soon."

She crossed her arms. "It's just not sensitive parenting."

"Eh, I disagree," Jason argued, cocking his head. "In a couple years' time he'd have learned the truth anyway, from friends and even teachers."

Mila flung her neck back. "Ugh, I'd never tell my fourth graders that Santa doesn't exist." Her eyes grew big. "Some still believe."

"Anyway, the father had a defense."

"But a poor one! He was permitted to self-study since he was already a parent on foreign territory. He passed the Parenthood Competency Test and took the Parenthood Oath of Office—but he conveniently claimed he was ignorant of the Coolbeensian Bill of Rights."

"Figures." Jason kept his hands in a steeple position. "He hadn't yet become accustomed to the laws of the land, including the Bill of Rights."

"Everyone, immigrant or not, should know their rights and those of others. The defendant claimed he broke the law out of ignorance. He can't use ignorance of the law as a defense," Mila exclaimed. "Laws are in place for all citizens, whether they know them or not. This *father*," she muttered with an ugly curl of her lips, "had a responsibility to find out about his new country's laws, all of which were publicly accessible."

"I still don't think there's sufficient evidence," Jason said, shaking his head.

"What d'you mean? Judge Eloney's decision to convict the parent for violating the child's Fifth Amendment right was based on sufficient evidence."

"Judge Eloney? I thought he was President Eloney."

"He is. Didn't you hear him at the parade? President Eloney is Coolbeensia's judicial system too."

Jason stared incredulously at the opposite wall. "Hmm. No, I didn't hear. A multitasker who runs the country and the courts. Impressive." He looked back at Mila. "Anyway, what evidence?"

"An innocent child's devastation is enough evidence of a violation," Mila huffed. "The defendant's conduct speaks for itself."

She looked intently at the father of her future children. "Put yourself at the scene. Don't just read the case. Bring it to life," she implored, making expansive gestures with her arms. "Consider that if we pass the ultimate test and have kids, you'll encounter this situation at some point."

113

"Okay, well, if I were the father, I'd, uh, probably want to avoid upsetting my son like that."

"Exactly. The verdict is just." Mila fell back against the sofa. "The defendant was sentenced to two seasons of traveling with his son on the Santa Railway. I support the ruling. Scenic holiday train rides are fully capable of restoring the loss of wonder the poor kid experienced."

She clasped her hands behind her head. "Judge Eloney made the right decision."

Throwing her legs up one by one on the coffee table, she said, "I can't wait to analyze this case in class."

"And hear how everyone else deciphered it?"

"Yep. It'll be interesting to hear the opinions of our potential future parent comrades." She winked at her husband.

Chapter 16

Mila's Coolbeensian worldview opened that Saturday as she and Vera joined up for a spectacular Taste of Coolbeensia food tour. The lengthy walking tour would take them through the heart of the micronation and back so their tastebuds had a chance to explore its finest worldly fare.

Stephania and Ada, the president's twins, who served as the ministers of ethnic food tours, personally guided them among a large group of food aficionados. Apparently, being everyday tour guides wasn't beneath their remarkable positions at the distinguished Office of the President.

The twenty-two-year-olds were spitting images of not only each other but their quirky father, except for the ladies being taller, more strikingly elegant, and a bit further up on the scale of normalcy.

Ten o'clock arrived in no time. "Keep your minds and mouths open, because today we'll be visiting the restaurants, bakeries, pubs, and farms that give our splendid micronation its unique blend of sumptuous flavors," Stephanie announced through a red bullhorn.

Ada, the more outgoing of the two, made her statement immediately after with sweeping gestures and a bright-eyed gaze. Her extroverted personality more closely resembled Eloney's than her sister's. "Ladies and gentlemen, you'll have the privilege to meet Coolbeensia's most distinguished culinary chefs, brewmasters, farmers, restauranteurs, and bakers on our day-long tour. I hope you've got your good walking shoes on and a hungry tummy. Let's start this exciting food tour extravaganza!" Ada motioned with her hand for the group to follow.

The excursion first took them to a South Korean street vendor serving foods popular in K-dramas. "Here we get a taste of cornflake-coated corndogs and cheese sticks. Pick your flavor," Stephanie announced to members of the tour, who ranged from twenty-somethings to fanny-pack-wearing women and men who appeared in the midst of retirement.

Mila watched the food vendor dip a cheese stick, the length of a US dollar bill, into a vat of gooey rice flour batter, then roll it into a tray of cornflakes. She dropped the whole concoction into a deep fryer spattering with hot oil and pulled it out three minutes later.

"Here you are," the vendor said, handing the fried cheese stick to Mila.

She sprinkled sugar over the cheese stick and drizzled it with a honey mustard sauce, anticipating the mix of sweet and savory to surprise her tastebuds. Vera received a cooked cheese stick at the same time. Mila toasted hers with Vera's and, summoning her adventurous side, took a huge bite.

"Mm-mm!" The cheese stretched a foot long from Mila's mouth as she extended her arm.

"Delicious," Vera said. "Back home in China, we're not big on cheese. But this tastes amazing."

Mila nodded, her mouth full of fried cheese and sweet rice dough.

"Coolbeensia is rich in culinary delights from cultures all over the world, thanks to my dad's open-door immigration policy. Ada and I will continue taking you through our cosmopolitan micronation to experience more of the finest flavors found nowhere else in a single place." Stephanie, in her floral drawstring pants and pink summer tank top, led the way.

"Name any unique culture in the world, and Coolbeensia likely serves its cuisine," Ada boasted, flipping her long hair back. "We're proud to say these exciting dishes are all right here in downtown alone."

Mila and Vera followed their dedicated tour guides through the streets, stopping at a corner pub and speaking to the brewmaster. His dark, scraggly beard hung over his plaid, navy-blue shirt as he discussed how he assembled menus, invented brand-new dishes, and designed the brewery. Vera and Mila toasted again, this time with glass beer mugs full of frothy beer.

The group traveled to the heart of downtown and stopped by a Greek restaurant. Meaty aromas filled the air. The mustached restauranteur with a jiggling belly and a generous nature offered them sizzling kebabs on a stick with miniature tubs of freshly made tzatziki sauce for dipping. "Opa!" Mila exclaimed.

A crowded Mexican bakery was next. The tour group managed to fit inside and have a taste of fluffy, soft conchas. The smiling baker in her white apron described her process for making the breakfast treat, remarking that it was especially delicious when served with a mug of hot cocoa.

Mila stood up front, listening to her methods and taking mental notes.

Four hours after it started, the tour wound down at a Cuban eatery in the middle of town. Mila took a seat at a table for two on the outdoor patio. The hum of conversations and vibrant green plants surrounded her and Vera as they gave their dessert orders from underneath a bright-red canopy.

"A sweet indulgence seems to be the perfect way to end the tour," Mila said, snapping the menu closed.

Vera nodded and handed her menu back to the waiter.

Within a few minutes, Mila's Cuban flan arrived, topped with two raspberries and a mint leaf.

"So, how're you doing in class?" Mila asked, as she dug her spoon into the luscious milky dessert.

Vera swirled her arroz con leche. "It's a lot to take in. I've been studying every night and feel okay about my progress. It's Tim I'm worried about," she said, bringing a spoonful of the sweet rice pudding to her mouth. "He's more concerned about what's streaming in baseball."

"Oh, my." Mila's gaze dropped.

"I hear the highest score ever received on the Parenthood Competency Test is an 85."

"It's a hard test," Mila added, her shoulders curling. "What bothers me is that it's graded on a curve."

Vera didn't flinch. "I'd expect it to be, since students come from diverse backgrounds and with different academic abilities."

"Sure, but grading on a curve means scores are lowered enough so that a percentage of students fail. If the whole class performs well, everyone will pass." She absentmindedly bathed the soft flan in the golden syrup. "But my concern is Peter."

Vera glanced up. "Him, yeah. He never seems to pay attention. He's worse than Tim."

"Peter needs to do well enough to pass. Our grades are based on our peers' performances, which makes him a threat to our scores on the Parenthood Competency Test at the end of the term." The metal spoon slipped from her fingers, producing a cacophonous *clank* against the porcelain plate.

"I guess all you really need to do is pass the test. The final grade doesn't matter much," Vera said.

Shaking her head, Mila dabbed the corners of her mouth with her cloth napkin. "My test grade is important to me. A high score opens the doors to more opportunities."

"Really? Like what?"

Mila leaned forward across the table. "I aspire to join the Coolbeensian Professional Parent Guild."

"Hmm. Never heard of it. But then again, I'm a new immigrant."

"We both are." Mila reached out her hand and rested it on Vera's for a second. "In a nutshell, it's a progressive association that promotes excellence in parenting. It unites Coolbeensian parents. As an influential force, it works in the service of all children by protecting their natural-born rights, like unconditional care. The guild is the conscience of the parenting profession."

"How do grades influence joining it?" Vera tilted her head to one side.

As she rolled the importance of rank off her tongue, Mila's heart beat faster. "A high grade is proof that I can apply the lessons. It shows I understand the complex material taught at the Parenthood Polytechnic and that I have the essential ability to think critically."

"Hmm. And I always thought undergrad courses did that."

Mila's muscles clenched at her jawline. "I need to show the guild that I have the level of knowledge to be successful in the field of professional parenting. And I can do that by scoring high. In fact, the guild won't even look at me if haven't earned an impressive grade on the Parenthood Competency Test."

"Sounds strict."

"It's a reasonable criterion." Mila leaned against the back of the patio chair. "High grades ensure the best possible members are doing the work. It opens the doors to leadership positions in the guild. It's something I strive for." She bit her bottom lip. "A good grade on the PCT is the chief indicator of how serious a mother or father is about the parenting profession."

Mila rubbed her face, let her chin fall into her hands, and stared out vacantly into the distance. "My biggest worry is Peter's lack of enthusiasm. I don't want him pulling my grade down and crushing my ambitions."

"You know," Vera offered, "we could form a study group and invite him and Amelia. It'd be a way to get him to focus on the assignments."

"Or even do them in the first place." Mila contemplated her suggestion for a minute. "It could work." Having like-minded friends always led to the right answers. She perked up and smiled. "I think it's a great idea, Vera. I'll invite them next class."

Chapter 17

"Study group?" Peter exclaimed, throwing his head back, as if he'd never heard of the concept before and was offended by the mere suggestion.

"Yeah." Mila maintained her equanimity. Trying to hold a conversation with someone as distractable and flighty as Peter was expected to be a challenge. "We talk through concepts the professor introduces in class and support each other's study efforts." She spoke of *efforts* nonchalantly, but her chest felt ripped open by the fact that Peter didn't put forth anything of the sort.

"But it's not a replacement for studying on your own," she added. "It's a supplement." She studied his half-hearted shrugging, his emotionless stare, and his flat response—his characteristic indifference.

Peter's jock-like body sagged in the classroom chair where he'd sat during class, which had just finished. Mila had snagged him before he bolted out the door.

"If you have questions about hypotheticals, members of our study group can help answer them. It's a great place to flesh out your analyses of cases."

"Eh, I dunno."

Peter's expression looked exactly like the one he showed in class—unenthused, unconcerned, and on the verge of dropping dead from boredom.

"It's sure to increase your chances of passing the Parenthood Competency Test at the end of the term."

"Oh?" His posture perked up.

She was making progress, albeit painfully slow, almost like teaching a child to eat with cutlery.

"I dunno. Classes take everything outta me. Then put a study group on top of that?"

He had a glazed look in his eyes.

"There's a lot of pressure, definitely, on all of us. But it's up to you. You surely have questions about your professional parenting education. If they're not answered by Professor Wigglebun, maybe some of us can pitch in."

She'd done her part. Mila stood up and gathered her belongings. Jason was in the car. She didn't want to leave him waiting too long. "Anyway, I'll be bringing the chips, soda, and sandwiches. So—"

Peter raised an eyebrow. He licked his lips. "Uh, what time again?"

"Thursday evenings at seven o'clock, until we approach the Parenthood Competency Test. Then, a month before the test, we'll go full-force and hold them twice weekly." Turning to him, she said with a smile, "Maybe we'll see you there."

Mila hurried out the door, hoping her dreams of joining the Coolbeensian Professional Parent Guild wouldn't be stymied by her grossly unmotivated classmate.

Mila and Jason sat around the table with Vera, Tim, and Simon in an empty classroom.

"Isn't Kaya coming?" Mila asked Simon.

Fidgeting, he tugged at his shirt collar. "Nah, she's out clubbing with the girls."

"Oh." Mila bit her lower lip.

Clasping her hands under her chin, she addressed her study group. "Well, we better get started if we want to make it home on time." She looked over at Jason. "What's on the agenda?"

He shuffled a few papers before settling on one. "Contracts, in other words, what Coolbeensian law will enforce. As we all know, birth creates an automatic contract between parent and child. We'll also look at the remedies for breaches of contract as well as parental nonperformance." He glanced around at the group. "Anyone want to take the first stab?"

Vera, leaning forward, jumped in. "Cases of parental nonperformance involve avoiding rules and limits."

"How'd you go from a laid-back parenting style all the way to nonperformance?" Tim argued with a narrowing of his eyes. He seemed peeved.

His wife glared back at him. "It's not laid-back. Children need rules. Without them, they're bound to have horrible temper tantrums and defy every adult they meet. Haven't you been paying attention in class?"

Tim rolled his eyes and swiped his phone from his back pocket. He started browsing through it, clearly neglecting any further discussion.

Sensing the tension between them, Mila quickly changed the topic. "Balancing family and work life is also a key way to avoid nonperformance in child-rearing and preserve the elements of the contractual agreement."

"There's tons of resources," Simon noted. He relaxed in his chair, his limbs loose and his features softened. He appeared unmoved by his girlfriend's no-show. "Parents don't need to feel ashamed just asking for a hand. Otherwise, we'd end up neglecting either our kids or our careers."

"Parenting is the career," Jason chimed in.

"Yep, it's going to be our profession." Mila grinned. "One of two for busy Coolbeensian moms and dads."

"And one of those careers lasts eighteen years. More often for life. Talk about tenure," Jason joked.

"It's the one most satisfying career that doesn't pay the bills," Mila said, her voice bubbly.

"Rather, it increases the bills!" Jason threw his head back, laughing at his own humor.

In the midst of their lighthearted banter, the door swung open. Peter waltzed inside. "Hey."

"Welcome," Mila greeted him cheerfully. "Glad you came. Have a seat."

"Don't mind if I do." Peter plopped down next to the table of food. "Right here."

"Where's Amelia?" Vera asked.

"She's sittin' at home eatin' her tub of rocky-road ice cream with a plate of pickles." His eyes grew wide. "Lots of pickles: pickled eggs, pickled okra, pickled beets."

Vera gave Mila a strange glance.

The newest member of the study group helped himself to two soda cans, a bag of chips, and a hot dog.

"Hey, I thought you said you was bringin' sandwiches?" Peter asked.

"I did."

"Hot dogs ain't sandwiches," he shot back.

"Of course they are. They're meat stuffed in between bread. Sandwiches," she scoffed. "It's like you're saying tomatoes aren't fruit."

With a harsh squint, he snapped, "They aren't."

"Huh, from a strictly biological point of view, tomatoes are, but from a prosocial one, they aren't." She stared Peter down. "What's more important, biology or sociability, in the context of parenthood class?"

"That's a trick question." He put back the hot dog and ripped open his bag of chips.

"Let's get back to studying." After her little tête-à-tête with Peter, Mila had already begun to feel exhausted. "We'll move on to negligence that violates Coolbeensian law."

Peter crunched the chips so loudly that the other students shot glances at him. Mila, too, couldn't help but feel perturbed by his obnoxious munching sounds.

He recoiled and spat out the chips. "Yuck! I thought you said you was bringin' chips?"

Unnerved by his second inappropriate outburst, Mila felt herself being tested. "Those *are* chips."

He turned the package around. "It says here they're veggie chips." His mouth dropped. "Veggie chips? They aren't *real* chips!" He looked at her like she'd just served him cherry gelatin salad.

Mila glowered at him. "Do you realize you're having a tantrum right here?"

Growing red in the face, he held his breath, then snapped. "Don't tell me what I'm having and what I'm not having. I'll be the judge of that."

"You know, Peter, my fourth graders are more mature than you," Mila grumbled.

"You insultin' me?" Peter demanded, cracking his knuckles. "Comparin' me to fourth graders?"

"Your aggressive attitude is not appreciated," Mila shrieked. "Your refusal to take this job seriously offends me." By now, she found herself standing, her palms placed firmly on the desk.

As the others looked on with a loss for words, she continued her harangue. "As a professional parent student, you don't have time for squabbles like this."

"I got better things to do than study," he clapped back.

"Really? Like what?" Mila folded her arms across her chest.

"Like workin' on my sales, marketing, customer satisfaction, and accounting—all things that go into entrepreneurship."

"Whatever." She dropped into her seat. Her words came out choked with emotion. "You know, this fight is worth it, because it's practical experience for when a child screams at a parent, which, by the way, none of my fourth graders ever do. It's life experience I'd never get anywhere else. Humph!"

Jason put a hand on Mila's arm. At her husband's gentle touch, she realized she was involved in a fighting match she didn't want to be in. She took several long, deep breaths.

Mila composed herself, remembering she was the one who invited a rascal like Peter in the first place. She had to be the adult amid this unsettling immaturity. After all, her future was at stake.

"Okay, okay, let's just be cooperative and professional instead of hostile and juvenile. We ought to work together since we'll be seeing each other frequently at parent-teacher conferences, the playground, and while dropping the kids off at daycare."

"Eh, suit yourself," Peter said, crumpling the foil bag of chips and tossing it over his shoulder.

She shook her head and muttered, "Let's just focus on what we're here for."

Chapter 18

The next few months sped by, with Mila's schedule full of her teaching responsibilities, classes, extracurricular activities, and leading the study group. But her study groups weren't as effective as anticipated, due to one particularly slacking member.

"I'm sick of him," Mila screamed, as soon as she banged the door to their apartment shut. She'd slammed it so hard that the wintry pine wreath hanging outside fell, sending the red velvet bow, frosty winterberries, and a half-dozen plastic candy canes splattering on the hallway floor.

Ignoring the minor upheaval, she undid her coat buttons in rapid sequence. Too consumed by fury to hang it up properly, she flung it over the couch. It landed, then slowly slid onto the carpet.

"Calm down. It's only a few more months until the test. We're almost at the finish line."

Jason did his best to comfort his frazzled wife, but it was no use.

Mila crossed her arms tightly across her chest, plonked on the couch with a huff, and turned her scowling face away from her husband. "I have a mind to kick him out of the study group."

"The pressure's mounting. That's all. We're three months away from the biggest exam of our lives." He sauntered into the kitchen. "You're just feeling the stress."

Still seething, Mila sat muttering. "His altercations will undoubtedly affect his moral fitness character assessment for the PCT." She huffed and puffed. "I mean, there's no way he'll practice parenthood with good moral character. He doesn't have a moral bone in his body. I don't see him cleaning up his actions anytime in the near future either to show himself fit enough to practice."

"I hear ya," Jason yelled from the kitchen. He returned a couple of minutes later with a mug, out of which hung a tea bag string. "No doubt about it." He handed it to her. "Here, a warm cup of tea to soothe you."

She took it, immediately relaxing from the warmth of the mug.

After a few sips, she let out a huge breath. Jason sat in the recliner.

"No, I'm serious, Jason. Peter should be kicked out of the study group. He's too disruptive. All he does is pick fights with me." Her expression tightened again. "And he doesn't bother to fight anyone else."

Jason looked at his wife steadily. His tender gaze was bolstering. He reached his hand out, laying it on her knee. "He's intimidated. You're doing well, and he's not."

Mila burst into rambling mode, flailing an arm in the air. "I can't take it. His insufferable bickering every week is distracting. Me, Vera, Simon, and you—we're all trying to do our best to focus on the material, and Peter interferes. Seemingly intentionally. It's not all right that he keeps taking jabs at me." Clenching her teeth, she uttered, "I want him out."

"Okay. If you feel strongly about it, I support you. We'll discuss it with the rest of the group."

By mid-December, Peter was thrown out of Mila's study group.

"You got kicked out?" Amelia, nearing the end of her second trimester, asked, wide-eyed. "You must've done somethin' awful."

"I didn't do nothin'! This ain't fair." Peter kicked the loose scraps of wrapping paper that his girlfriend had thrown aside after wrapping presents.

"What do we do now?"

"I ain't gonna stand for this. No one kicks out Peter Losor." This was an insult he was bound to overcome the right way. His eyes squinted. A devilish grin spread across his face. He turned to Amelia, rubbing his palms together slowly. "I know just what we'll do." He threw his head back and laughed hideously.

"Come on," he said, grabbing Amelia's hand and whisking her out of the apartment.

"Where are we going?"

"To the library." His gaze was alert, his jaw set.

Within minutes, they'd arrived at the Parenthood Polytechnic's four-story library.

"Wow," Amelia exclaimed. "I'd never been inside an impressive place like this. Just look at all the chandeliers, the high ceilings, and—" She wriggled her nose. "Ew, the stale smell of books!"

Peter grunted as he pulled her along, down the aisle of desk after desk.

The two meandered through the multitude of rows of solid wood shelves stacked with thick, identical-looking books on parenting and Coolbeensian law as it pertained to raising children.

"How does anyone tell one book from the other? They all look the same." Amelia seemed dazed.

"Ugh, who knows," came Peter's terse reply.

"What are we looking for?" she asked, panting as they sojourned to the second floor.

"The most current study aids." Peter scanned the titles, up and down.

"What's a study aid?"

He looked at his girlfriend, pathetic and helpless, yet the mother of his future child. "Eh, they come in all forms: guides, treatises, pamphlets with examples and explanations."

His eyes gleamed as he picked out a slender title. "Hey, look here, it's the *Acing the Resz Parenthood Polytechnic* series. Just what we need." He shoved it into Amelia's hand.

Before she could question him, he collected all twenty-eight books in the series and stuffed them into Amelia's arms until she couldn't carry any more.

"What're we gonna do with these?" she asked, juggling the books in her full arms.

"You'll see. Follow me." Peter led her to the third floor.

They entered a quiet study area filled with comfy chairs next to little side tables, elongated desks, lamps, and computers. A spectacled librarian walked stiffly from one end to the other.

"Keep an eye on her," Peter whispered.

"What for?"

"Shh!"

Their footsteps barely made a sound as they stole across the blue low-pile carpet.

His shoulders hunched over, he crept silently to a tall bookshelf. "Psst! Over here."

Amelia waddled over. "These books are getting heavy," she whispered loudly.

"Put 'em on the shelf."

"But it's the wrong shelf," she cried out.

"Exactly. Those fools in the study group ain't never gonna find 'em," Peter cackled, bouncing on his toes.

The next day, Peter posted anonymously to the Parenthood Polytechnic's online forum.

Sitting at the computer, he typed, "Ho-hum knowledge of the parenthood profession is enough. U don't need no license." Before he clicked enter, he asked Amelia to proofread it.

"What're you asking me for? I ain't got a clue," she retorted.

"Fine. Here's an easier one: 'It's always a good idea to take parental advice from a non-licensed parent.'"

She giggled. "Sounds good to me."

He hit send.

"This one's pretty obvious." He pointed to a new entry: "The best place to find solutions to parenting problems is on the internet—not school. Everything's true on the internet." He hit return without bothering to consult Amelia.

He continued his posts in rapid-fire. "Don't be fooled. The Coolbeensian Bill of Rights lives in a void. There ain't no parental precedents to consider."

He chuckled as he submitted his final post of the day: "Interpreting the Coolbeensian Constitution literally is a wise move."

Over the next several weeks, Peter infiltrated the forum with inaccuracies and misleading posts. He leaned back, smiling with satisfaction after each hour's worth of hard work.

A group project came up in class, giving Peter an opportunity he couldn't resist. "Hey, did y'all hear from the online forum that it's a good idea to interpret the Coolbeensian Constitution literally?"

Simon knitted his brows. "Really?"

"Yep!"

Mila interrupted. "Don't listen to him. He's giving you wrong advice."

Peter shut up for ten minutes.

"Peter, if you're going to slack off and not contribute, it makes the rest of us do more work," Mila pointed out, as he sagged in his seat, staring blankly at the ceiling.

"Uh, you're right."

He straightened his posture and asked a question, then, a minute later, another. For the entire duration of the project, Peter yakked nonstop, asking question after question, in an attempt to contribute as he should.

Vera eyed Mila, who cried out, "Peter, your constant questions are irksome. We can't absorb the lessons if you keep hindering the process with your incessant chattering." Pinching her thumb and index finger in front of her, she exploded, "We're this close to taking the PCT, and you're blowing it for all of us!"

Peter squinted and gave her a hard smile.

Mila returned home that night, cursing under her breath.

"You know, I think Peter's been doing this on purpose all these months."

"What d'you mean?" Jason asked.

"I'm sure it was him who misfiled all the study aids in the library. And based on the ungrammatical wording, I'm sure he's behind all the incorrect advice in the online forums. He keeps asking silly questions, things he should know, to prevent the class from moving forward at this critical time."

She sighed. "Ever since I kicked him out of the study group, he's been engaged in sabotage."

"What're you going to do?" Jason's voice expressed concern.

Mila rubbed her forehead. "Oh, I don't know. The exam is two weeks away. I'll focus on my grade, as that's most important to me. But maybe I'll gain favor with the guild for my extracurricular activities. I've also been networking to make friends who can vouch for me when I apply. I'm even a part of parenting clinics. They'll serve me well beyond earning my license to practice."

She paced the floor, wringing her hands.

Chapter 19

"Peter," Amelia said, waddling into the room and rubbing her full belly.

"Not now, Amelia." Peter didn't look up as he typed away at the computer.

"Peter," Amelia cried out.

"I said, not now!"

"*Peter!*" Amelia shrieked so loudly that the flowery decorative porcelain plate etched with the words, "That which does not get us caught makes us richer," came loose from the wall and crashed to the floor, breaking into a thousand shards.

He'd never heard her scream that loudly, not even when they chugged up the lift hill and plunged down at 120 miles per hour on the Daredevil roller coaster at the amusement park back in Kansas. It was a fierce ride not many Kansans could stomach.

His body stiffened, and he turned his head cautiously, his eyes glassy.

Still rubbing her belly, Amelia switched to a softer, feminine tone. "I think my water broke."

"Huh?"

Peter's eyes bulged. He squeezed them shut, processing what he'd just heard. Men didn't hear those five words spoken every day. He gawked at his girlfriend's wide belly. She barely showed beneath her extra-extra-large T-shirt. Yet, he couldn't ignore the news.

He leapt off the seat, grabbed her by the hand, and hurried her to the car. Adrenaline pumping through his body, he pressed on the gas, ran two red lights, swerved to avoid a pedestrian by a hair, and broke the 30 miles per hour speed limit to reach the Coolbeensian General Hospital ten minutes away.

"My girlfriend. She's . . . she's in labor," he told the front desk in between rapid breaths.

Immediately, the hospital staff brought out a wheelchair and Amelia plonked into it. They wheeled her to the obstetrics department, where she lay on a gurney, holding tightly onto Peter's sweaty hand. He stood beside her bed, avoiding a clear view. He'd heard horror stories from the guys back home and didn't want to be a deer in headlights or pass out amid the gore.

"Your contractions are getting closer together," the obstetrician attending to Amelia stated. "Don't be surprised if you feel nauseous or your legs start cramping. You may feel pressure on your back."

"Pressure? I'm on fire. I feel like I'm gonna die," Amelia shouted, gasping with her eyes wide open and her fist clutching Peter's shirt as he stood beside her, not knowing what to do or what to expect—other than a brand-new wee one. Fear shot through his system but Amelia's uncontrolled yelling gave him an even bigger fright. He'd never seen her this zany before. She was delirious even without an epidural.

"Just stay calm. The calmer you are, the easier your delivery will be," the doctor assured her. "Practice your breathing."

Her eyes staring at the ceiling like a zombie out of an old-time black-and-white movie, she shrieked, "Practice *what*?"

The doctor looked over at Peter. "I apologize for this awkward timing, but it is my professional duty to ask. Do you and your girlfriend have a license to practice?"

"License? Oh, you mean a parental one?"

"Yes, sir, that's exactly what I mean," the obstetrician replied matter-of-factly.

"Nah, see, the judge told us to go to parental school."

The doctor lowered his chin to his chest. "Oh, well, I see. We'll contact Judge Eloney on your behalf and see what he says." He assured Peter with a touch on his arm, "It's just protocol. We are in Coolbeensia, after all." He instructed the nurse on what to do.

The nurse left the room and returned five minutes later. "Doctor, Judge Eloney has granted an allowance to Mr. Losor and Ms. Bord since the Parenthood Competency Test is in one week. Their results will determine their fate."

"Very well. Thank you, Tanya." The doctor turned to Peter. "Did you hear that?"

"Sure did." Peter gulped.

Amelia began yelling, "It's gonna kill me!"

"Ah, it looks like the baby is on his way out." The doctor positioned himself.

Amelia pushed and pushed, gasping for air and howling the entire time that she wouldn't make it out alive.

Within minutes, the sound of crying, in addition to Amelia's, filled the delivery room.

"Look who we have here," the obstetrician said, holding the baby in his arms. He handed him to Amelia, who was dripping with sweat. She swept back her drenched hair.

Upon taking the baby, she cried out, "After all that, a boy?"

"Yes, Ms. Bord, a healthy baby boy." The physician removed his goop-covered surgical gloves. He left the room as the nurse took over.

"Peter, it's wailing!" Amelia dangled the baby a foot out in front of her.

"Put him on your chest," Peter said, instantly forgetting the ghastly sights, smells of blood and sweat, and ear-piercing shrieks in the delivery room. She'd done it. His girlfriend, though incapable of much, brought their son into the world. He felt his lungs expand as he watched her bring him to her chest.

"Just adorable." The nurse wiped the baby's head with a soft cloth. "What'll you name him?" she asked with a smile.

"Name it?" Amelia gave her boyfriend a blank look. "Oh, we haven't gotten that far."

Peter cleared his throat. "We'll call him Peter II."

Amelia stared at her boyfriend in seeming shock. "A second Peter? Good grief."

The new father bounced on his toes as he tucked his hands casually into his front jean pockets. "Yep!" He'd come up with his son's name right on the spot. Eh, there was nothing to this parenting thing.

The nurse gave the two new parents a skeptical look. Hesitating, she offered, "Well, if you need anything, just press that button." Then she walked out.

Upon arriving at their apartment several hours later, Amelia and Peter put their new son into the cradle for the rest of the evening.

Peter II started to cry once the clock struck midnight. Amelia, asleep in bed after her agonizing delivery, popped one eye open. Her face lay squished against the pillow, as drool trickled out of the corner of her mouth. She didn't rouse, but lay there. "Peter," she whispered, turning over to poke him. He snorted, then continued his raucous snoring. The baby cried unattended for a half hour.

Grunting, she hauled herself out of bed and trudged to the crib. "Shush! I'm trying to get some sleep."

The baby continued to cry. "Shush, I said!"

She grabbed the milk bottle off the night stand and fed him.

An hour later, Peter II started wailing again.

"Peter!"

Groggily, he awoke. "Wh-what's the matter?"

"It won't stop crying. I told it to shush, but it won't listen," she complained.

"You just get some rest."

"How can I when it keeps screaming?"

Peter sat up, exhaled, and dropped his hairy shoulders. "Right, sleep deprivation's torture." Barely awake, he looked around the dim bedroom and then grabbed a box of earplugs laying randomly on the nightstand. He offered them to her. "Use these."

Amelia turned the box over. "Earplugs? Um, okay." She opened the box and stuck one in each ear.

"But if you're fast asleep, who's gonna feed the baby?" Peter asked, mumbling with his eyes half closed.

"What?" she asked.

Peter pointed to both his ears.

"Oh." Amelia removed her earplugs.

He repeated his vital question over the sound of Peter II's relentless, high-pitched crying.

"I dunno. I just fed it. How many times d'ya have to feed a baby?"

Peter threw his hands up and groaned.

The rest of the night, plus the next eighteen years, promised to be very long.

Chapter 20

Mila's muscles twitched even before she awoke on the day of the Parenthood Competency Test. With her nerves jittering nonstop, she couldn't stomach a bite of breakfast. Instead, she dressed up in her latte-colored silk shirt paired with beige slacks—a savvy look that boosted her confidence.

Jason unbuttoned the top of his shirt as he drove with her to the Resz Parenthood Polytechnic, arriving at 9:30 a.m., a half hour before the test. Mila's insides didn't stop fluttering.

"Remember, focus, just focus," she repeated out loud, as she blew sharp breaths in and out in a determined effort to relax. She couldn't stop worrying about what she did and didn't know.

Jason stood seemingly calm outside the door to the exam room, while Mila paced the halls.

At 9:45, the testing room opened, and Mila and Jason took their seats. She made herself comfortable for the difficult four-hour test ahead. She brought out a Sudoku puzzle and began working on the numbers to take her mind off the exam and calm her nerves.

Precisely at 9:59, Peter and Amelia stomped through the door, bickering. Oil shone on their chins, foreheads, and necks. It was only the end of March, yet sweat marks drenched their baggy clothes.

"You shoulda left it with the neighbor," Amelia scolded. "Then we wouldn't have to pay for day care."

"Just forget about the whole thing." Peter rubbed what looked like a brand-new sling around his left arm.

He scanned the classroom, eyeing the students and the few empty desks, then plonked into a seat behind Mila.

At ten o'clock sharp, Professor Wigglebun entered, smartly dressed in a two-piece cross-woven navy-blue business skirt suit and matching kitten heels.

She tapped the mic on the podium. "Students, today is the first of two days of the Parenthood Competency Test. It will be grueling. But you will receive a lunch break in between the morning and the afternoon block."

She cleared her throat. "These past nine months of intense and deliberate study should've prepared you to pass the exam as competently and painlessly as realistically possible."

The professor looked each student in the eye as if they were on her radar. "Cheating is not allowed, and anyone who attempts to engage in unscrupulous behavior is unfit for the practice of parenting."

Amelia leaned over and whispered to Peter. "What's unscrupulous mean?"

Peter shushed her and looked forward.

"Coolbeensian parents are held to high ethical standards. You will be watched carefully so as to deter cheating and uphold the exam's integrity." The professor picked up her eyeglasses, hanging on a chain, and placed them on the bridge of her nose. She tapped a stack of test materials against the podium.

Professor Wigglebun began to pass out the test booklets. As she walked through the aisles in between the desks, like an armed guard ready to punish the slightest misstep, she announced in her characteristically firm tone, "This morning's exam includes seventy multiple-choice questions. You are expected to fill in the bubbles with the correct answers. The afternoon exam will be similar."

As she handed a booklet to Peter, her stern face showed no expression. "This exam will test your knowledge of various topics on parenting, the application of these topics, and your ability to think critically to arrive at solutions that nurture a child's growth and development."

Peter shook his jowls as if to try to shake away the final mounting of crushing pressure.

"This exam tests your understanding of the standards expected of the parenting profession. Subject areas include the Coolbeensian Bill of Rights, contracts, and others taught in class."

Professor Wigglebun walked back to the front. "You have exactly two hours to take the first portion of the exam. You may begin."

Mila pushed up her sleeves. She dropped her head, focusing on comprehending the questions in front of her. As she clutched the pencil tightly to fill in the answers, the whites of her knuckles shone.

Peter's squinting eyes darted left and right. His gaze landed up front on Professor Wigglebun, who sat immersed in scrolling through her tablet.

He quietly undid a strap from the sling around his arm and pulled out a piece of paper. He looked at the other students in the classroom. Everyone's heads were in their tests. Holding the folded sheet below the desk, he scanned the notes, making sure to keep the paper out of sight. Then he filled in the first thirty bubbles on the exam.

Once the notes were no longer of use for the remaining questions, he tucked them back into his sling.

Mila seemed to be feverishly filling in the bubbles with her pencil. He peered over her shoulder. It couldn't be more perfect. He had a clear view of a good portion of her answers. There was no better student than her to help him pass.

She wouldn't mind helping him. After all, that's why she invited him to the study group in the first place. She'd kicked him out, but bygones were bygones. He could let her insult go. In any case, Mila would certainly want to help a struggling parent like him.

Questions 31 through 45 were in clear sight from his carefully chosen vantage point behind the school's top student. He hastily filled in the bubbles while he had the chance.

Then Mila placed her right elbow on the desk and dropped her head into her hand. Her long, shiny brunette hair cascaded over her hand like a dam inappropriately built in an arid, no-go area. What was she doing? She had some nerve, blocking his view of the answers. Peter's face grew red. He clenched his teeth as steam nearly shot out of his ears.

He glanced up at the clock. Fifteen minutes left and he still hadn't filled in the last twenty-five answers. He grunted to himself. He should've gone with his crazy notion to pay a stand-in to take the test for him, but he reneged on the idea, since it was a small class and everyone was familiar with him.

He rushed to fill in the rest bubbles willy-nilly, though he had no clue.

Once the clock struck noon, Professor Wigglebun instructed the students to put down their pencils. She collected the exams and dismissed the students for lunch.

Peter didn't budge for a couple of minutes, though Amelia tugged at his arm. She finally gave up and headed toward the cafeteria. He sat in his chair, pressing his lips tightly into a grimace. He sighed heavily and shook his head. Slowly, he got up and ducked into the cafeteria with the rest of them.

An hour later, the students returned to finish the second portion of the test.

Day two of the test arrived, and the students filed into the exam room for the three-hour session. All of the test takers had brought their laptops and propped them open on their desks. Peter and Amelia did the same, plonking their old laptops on the desk. As Peter opened his, the internal fan produced a loud, disturbing whirring noise. The other students turned their heads back and looked at him.

"He-he," Peter laughed. "Can't ever throw away an old computer that still works, can ya?"

The students grunted and returned their gazes forward.

Just like the day prior, Professor Wigglebun passed out the test questions printed on paper. "The final portion of the Parenthood Competency Test is a demanding performance assessment intended to evaluate your application of real-life parental skills." She looked over the rim of her eyeglasses. "It may even be more exhausting than yesterday's test."

Peter squirmed in his seat.

"You will read past cases involving parents and children and provide coherent, reasoned analyses that factor in Coolbeensian precedents. Type in your answers in essay form on your laptops." She eyed the class with her hands resting on either side of the podium. "You have three hours. Your time starts now."

The students began typing away at rapid speed. The sounds of their collective tapping filled the room.

For Peter, the *tap-taps* were the sounds of impending doom.

Mila's laptop screen was in clear view—he'd made sure to sit in the same advantageous spot—but there was no way he'd successfully copy her answers. He'd be easily found out, since he only had time to copy them verbatim. His chances of passing this portion of the test were otherwise slim.

He had a decision to make.

He swallowed hard.

Chapter 21

Fragrant garlic, onions, and herbs infused the Brazilian steakhouse. The constant *pop-pop* sounds of steaks sizzling in the kitchen filled the cool dining atmosphere with lively music. Mila sat at a table with her husband, admiring the crystal vase holding fresh-cut flowers and the flames of the novelty candles flickering in the dimness.

"This place is beautiful." She and Jason hadn't had a night out in over nine months. She'd almost forgotten what it was like to savor a first-class dinner prepared by a professional gaucho chef. This evening, they decided to spoil themselves after their long, tiring stretch.

"Well-deserved though," Jason replied.

Mila looked around and caught sight of Vera's short black bob as she entered through the front door. Rising slightly off her seat, she gave her an enthusiastic here-we-are wave.

Vera smiled and sauntered over to join her and Jason.

"Smells delicious," Vera said, pulling her chair closer to the table. "And expensive."

"But we're worth it," Mila exclaimed, "as newly licensed parents!"

She leaned in to Vera and they giggled together like small children.

"I didn't dare open the email notification from the Coolbeensia Parenthood Board of Examiners." Vera placed her palm on her chest and rolled her eyes up to the ceiling. "I thought, what if I didn't pass? It would have shattered my world."

"Me too." Mila reached out to touch Vera's hand. "I asked Jason to open the email and tell me my results. Then I decided I wanted to know for myself. I braced for the worst and clicked. To my surprise, it was good news!" A flood of warm energy pulsed through her.

"If I'm not mistaken, you earned the highest score in the class, a 90 percent." Vera congratulated Mila as a dear friend would. "I'm thrilled you achieved your goal. You'll have no trouble getting into the Coolbeensian Professional Parent Guild."

Mila crossed her fingers. "I hope so. I haven't had time to apply yet, since we just got our results." She brought up her fingers and squeezed them in front of her face. "We're this close to achieving our dream of parenthood. Passing the Parenthood Competency Test changes everything for us."

"By the way, where's Tim?" Jason, asked, joining the bubbly conversation between the two ladies. He leaned back in his chair.

Vera's expression turned morose. She gave Mila a sidelong glance and slid her fingers up and down the stem of an empty wine glass. "Oh, he couldn't come. He didn't pass the test, and . . ."

"He didn't?" A look of genuine surprise crossed Mila's face. She never imagined Tim wouldn't pass. He'd come to the study group sessions, though he hardly contributed to their discussions.

"No, he, um, well, I told him I couldn't stay married to someone who didn't pass this very important exam. I want children more than anything, and he proves he can't be the father they deserve."

Mila placed her fingers on her open mouth.

"We're getting divorced."

Mila's shoulders dropped. A minute of silence passed. "Oh, Vera, I'm sorry. How do you feel about it?"

Vera sighed and lowered her gaze to her lap. "Don't be. It's for the best. I'm actually feeling good about it. The exam opened my eyes to the potential father Tim would've been. It saved us a lot more fights down the road. We haven't been on the best terms for a long time. Petty disagreements, big fights, throwing dishes against the wall, sleeping on the couch—the whole shebang."

Her dark eyes popped open and glistened under the subtle glow from the raindrop chandeliers. "But a few months ago, I met a man at a coffee shop on Main Street."

"Ooooh, you did?" Mila squealed, unable to stay still.

"We hit it off. Then I found out he passed the Parenthood Competency Test. It was the icing on the cake. He was already too perfect, but him revealing this vital criterion made him utterly irresistible. Mila," she said, grasping her hands with both of hers, "we're in love!"

"What great news!" Mila couldn't help but to share her friend's joy. A lightness flooded her limbs.

"Now that I've passed the exam, too, we've proven to each other that we can bring children into this world and raise them together with unconditional love."

"It's great to find someone who's on the same page as you." Mila gave her husband a flirtatious glance.

His chin high, Jason smiled back.

"We should order." Mila flipped open her à la carte menu. The costs of the prime cuts were in the upper double digits. She and Jason had agreed to splurge on themselves since they both passed the biggest test of their lives. The exorbitant prices didn't dissuade two committed professionals living on teachers' salaries from paying a premium for a high-quality celebration dinner.

"The prime aged ribeye sounds delish," Jason said.

"They promise an authentic churrasco experience." She licked her lips. "It says here the chefs serve us tableside, carving sumptuous meats from the skewers and dropping the fire-roasted pieces onto our plates." She fanned herself with the menu. "Ah, I'm dying for a bite."

As they perused the menus, Simon strolled into the restaurant.

"Hey, guys," he said, pulling out a seat.

"Simon! How'd it go?" Mila asked, wide-eyed.

His hunched posture and frown gave away everything. Mila didn't even have to ask.

"I-I didn't pass," Simon stuttered. Granted, he was the nervous sort, but upon collapsing into the seat and slinking to the edge, he seemed defeated.

"That's terrible," Mila said in a soothing voice, conveying sympathy as a friend would. Simon may not have been the brightest bulb in the class, but he was a good guy. He'd have been a decent parent.

"Yeah, but I'll be retaking the exam."

"You worked hard during our study groups," Mila said with an understanding nod. "I'm sure you'll pass next time."

"It was just nerves, that's all. I was too anxious; it did me in." Simon looked glum.

Mila did a quick turn toward the front door. "I didn't see Kaya come in with you. Actually, I don't think I saw her at the exam either."

Simon finally made eye contact. "That's because she wasn't there. She hopped over the border to New Mexico for a party. She met a guy there and left with him. She texted me we're done and I can do whatever I want." He shrugged. "That's the last I heard from her."

"She didn't seem too serious anyway," Mila said, trying to comfort him.

"About me or the exam?"

Mila took a contemplative pause.

Simon made a dismissive wave with his hand. "Never mind. It doesn't matter." He perked up. "What're we having for dinner? I could use a drink."

"Oooh, this succulent grilled shrimp sounds divine," Vera said.

"It's the prime aged ribeye for me." Jason snapped his menu shut. "Beautifully marbled and richly flavorful. Can't top that."

"Lamb steak. Hmm, never tried it. Guess it's time for new beginnings, huh?" Simon said, smiling for the first time that night.

Mila studied the menu a bit longer. "I think I'll have the prime filet mignon." She set down her menu. "It's wrapped in bacon. Mm-mm."

The waiter arrived, taking their orders.

Minutes later, the waiter returned with their drinks.

"Let me propose a toast. To future professional parenthood." Mila toasted her blueberry spiced mojito with Jason's East Side Manhattan. Vera and Simon raised their glasses of vodka martinis. The friends ate and drank heartily and chatted well into the late evening hours.

Chapter 22

Peter strolled down the winding park path with his hands half tucked into the front pockets of his distressed blue jeans. Amelia strode next to him, pushing a stroller with Peter II napping inside.

The temperate spring weather drew them outside, out of their cramped garden apartment where they'd hibernated. Trees blossomed with green leaves and tiny pink-and-white buds, many of which had fallen onto the paved path, creating a soft floral carpet.

"I don't get it. That test was awful, just awful," Amelia whined, clenching her teeth.

"Yep," was all Peter could muster.

Baby squirrels darted to and fro, picking up fallen buds from the sugar maple trees lining the path.

"Some of those multiple-choice questions were half baked." Her eyes darted this way and that, as joggers

161

wearing long-sleeved layers jogged past, huffing and puffing. "I mean it's pretty obvious love and trust are rewards, not rights."

Peter grunted as he casually ambled, breathing in the fresh air and the unmistakable scents of spring. The blossoms released subtle, sweet scents, which put him in a relaxed mood—a mood he hadn't enjoyed for more than nine months.

"One true and false question had me wondering what blockhead wrote up this test. It asked if it's good parenting to hit and scream." Amelia flinched her head back. "What a silly question. How else would we make children behave?"

Peter wiggled his nose. He knew better than to interrupt when she was on a roll.

"Then it had me guessing all over again." She forced an ugly twist of her mouth, as if ridiculing the writer of the abominable test. "It asked, 'Do you believe empathy is better than no empathy?' I wrote, 'No comprende Greek.' I thought this test was supposed to be in English. No wonder it was so hard."

Peter rolled his eyes and sighed.

The couple kept walking, taking in the sights and sounds of Coolbeensia's pristine natural park areas. The grass was well-manicured, even giving off an earthy scent like it was freshly cut. The thick Leyland cypress hedges bordering one side of the path stood neatly trimmed. Not a single crumpled ball of litter or crushed soda can lay in their way.

The immaculateness and orderliness of Coolbeensia struck Peter. He rather liked it. It was a far cry from growing up in Unibrowumbia or even living in Kansas for that matter. He compared it to living in a well-maintained mansion versus a rickety, old shack. The distinctness was like night and day, and he was getting accustomed to it. No one would pick a run-down shack over a palatial mansion.

"Then the essay part stumped me. How do they get away with asking stupid questions?" Amelia scratched at her cheek. "It asked, 'What are your views on corporal punishment?'"

A woman in a light blue raincoat strolled toward them.

"I answered that if corporals are right for the army, it works on children just the same."

The woman threw a mean glance at Amelia and curled her lips as she walked by.

Amelia grabbed Peter's arm as she stared at her with bulging eyes. The woman passed a few yards behind them. She whipped her head of silvery-brown hair back around and whispered, "Did you see that lady give me that dirty look? People are so inconsiderate."

Peter yawned, kept his vacant gaze ahead, and maintained his leisurely pace. His girlfriend could go on and on, with or without him contributing to the conversation. It was best more often than not to keep his mouth shut whenever she opened hers.

"And some of the questions made no sense. It asked

whether or not you believe in praising achievements."

"What'd ya answer?" he finally asked, merely out of curiosity, as he scratched his stubbly chin.

"I wrote, of course—if they're worth praising, like doing good in the family business, which my boyfriend calls *entrepreneurship*."

Peter slapped his forehead with his palm, then rubbed his cheek. He squeezed his eyes shut for a few seconds before opening them and thinking absolutely nothing— which Amelia must've done for the entire duration of the two-day test.

"And then it asked, 'Can you set a good example for a child?'" Amelia slowly swiveled her head, glancing at her surroundings. "*That* was a no-brainer. I wrote that I'm a great example for everyone."

"Jeez," Peter mumbled under his breath as he looked the other away.

"Ya know," Amelia started, sounding as sincere as she could be, "I can't understand why we failed the Parenthood Competency Test. The whole thing was nothin' but baloney."

Peter shook his head. He'd failed miserably, having earned lower than the minimum passing score, despite having gotten a hefty number of the right answers from the smartest student in class. It must've been the essay portion that pulled down his score as easily as an avalanche tore down trees in its path.

His feet kicked at the ground.

What a life-changing bummer. Now he'd have to face the consequences—as Judge Eloney put it, their "results will determine their fate." He had yet to find out exactly what that fate would be. But he'd hear from the court soon. He shivered. Whatever the judge decided, he wasn't going to like it.

A light rain started to fall.

"Oh, look, a drizzle." Amelia looked up and flattened out her palm as the raindrops splashed on it.

"We better get going."

"Why?"

"It looks like it's gonna storm," Peter answered with a slight groan. "Our son will catch a cold."

"A little rain never hurt no one. It'll be fine." Amelia gave a dismissive wave of her hand as she pushed the stroller with the other. "I don't wanna be cooped up in that little apartment."

Thunder clapped in the distance. A bright flash of lightning lit up the darkened sky beyond the park.

Amelia jumped. "Oh, my."

The light rain gradually turned into a heavy downpour.

Passersby left and right ran for cover, pulling their spring jackets over their heads. The sounds of big, pattering raindrops and the stomps of feet pounding against the ground lent a strangeness to the darkened atmosphere.

Peter grabbed the handlebars to the stroller and pushed fast. He had to get himself and his son out of the fierce, oncoming storm.

"Hey!" Amelia shouted as she waddled behind, trying to catch up.

It didn't take long for Peter to roll down the path and back to the parking lot. He put Peter II into the car seat. Heavily panting, Amelia opened the car door and slid inside.

At the red light, Peter reached into the back seat and put his hand on his son's forehead. "Looks like he's got a temperature."

"A temperature of what?"

"Darlin', all I'm sayin' is that he's too warm."

"Oh, we'll just give it an aspirin when we get home." Amelia looked casually out the passenger-side window and clapped her hands. "Problem solved."

Peter narrowed his eyes and clutched the steering wheel tighter. No one gives a one-month-old aspirin. And no one was giving *his* baby an aspirin.

Torrents of rain pounded against the windshield, mimicking the steady thumping sounds of conga drums beating in times of war. Driving through this storm was like taking the car through a sudsy conveyor car wash, with little visibility and distractions from the brushes whirling maniacally on either side. He turned on his wipers full force. The worn blades swished back and forth rapidly, squeaking annoyingly against the glass because they were overdue for a replacement.

An oncoming car sped past the red light on the slippery roadway. Peter hastily turned the steering wheel at the last second, his wheels screeching loudly, avoiding a disastrous head-on collision.

His child started wailing nonstop in the back seat.

Amelia kept yelling at their son at the top of her lungs to shush.

Peter had a mind to pull out his hair, but his hands were busy gripping the steering wheel.

Gadzooks! What was he going to do?

Chapter 23

"You almost ready, honey?" Mila shouted as she poked the back of her silver dangle hoop earring through her left earlobe. She gave herself one last look in the mirror, straightening out the creases of her blue-and-white patterned dress topped with a puffy blue bowknot tie.

Dressing to the nines for the ceremony was a must. She'd picked out a new dress precisely for this honorable occasion. It had to express her respect for her prestigious new role as a licensed parent. Besides, she'd be in the company of other newly licensed parents, all draped in their finest for this once-in-a-lifetime event. She aimed to show up at her best.

Jason emerged from the bathroom, tugging at the cuffs of his pressed white dress shirt under his tan jacket. "Ready as I'll ever be," he yelled back.

Mila hurried down the hall and slipped on her blue heels. Her husband smelled luxurious, like notes of woody rosewood with a hint of spicy sandalwood. He must've dabbed on the cologne she'd given him as a gift for passing the Parenthood Competency Test. She'd definitely married the sexiest man on earth.

She let out a quick breath and gave her husband a smile. "Let's do this."

A fifteen-minute drive later, they arrived at a small, white banquet hall designed in the style of neoclassical architecture. With its two white columns and multiple arched windows, it was the most beautiful building she'd seen in Coolbeensia—and for good reason. It was here that newly licensed parents got their start. The hall laid the foundation for generations of well-nurtured, productive, and happy citizens.

Mila and Jason hopped up the four steps and pulled the door open. They were greeted by numerous round tables covered in pleated white cloths that hung to the yellow floral carpet. White seat covers blanketed all the chairs. Wine glasses, white napkins folded in perfect white triangles, stacked plates, and silverware sat on the tables, ready to be utilized.

Waiters in white jackets, black bowties, and black slacks stood near the walls, as if awaiting the moment their professional services would be needed.

Men and women dressed in dapper suits and feminine dresses socialized in the hall along with Mila and Jason. Their faces, giving off the sheen of accomplishment, expressed jubilation, certainly for having passed the Parenthood Competency Test. Mila knew the feeling, as every fiber of her being radiated with joy. She felt a connection with the crowd and shared their happiness.

Vera walked over from the other side, leading a gentleman in a sleek blue suit by the hand.

"Mila," she said, embracing her, "I'd like you to meet Bao." Vera's voice sounded chipper and bright. "I told you all about him."

"You certainly did." Mila turned to Bao and extended her hand. "Vera has mentioned some wonderful things about you."

"Oh, has she?" he said upon shaking it. "Well, she's the wonderful one."

Vera pinched Bao's arm. "Oh, stop. You're too fantastic."

He leaned into her. "No, you are."

They both giggled like best friends at the playground.

Looking into Bao's brown eyes and clearly tuning out the rest of the world, Vera said dreamily, "We met over an espresso and bonded over countless long macchiatos."

"And the latte art sealed the deal." Bao chuckled.

Vera reached out her arm and touched Mila's. "He's referring to the foam hearts the barista designed on our coffees."

The rapport between them was magical. Vera had finally found the perfect future co-parent.

"Looks like the ceremony is about to start," Jason interrupted.

Vera and Bao took their seats on the opposite side.

Jason pulled out a chair for Mila. She nestled into the soft cushion. Her husband took his seat as several others joined them at the table. Soon, guests packed the hall—not one chair stood empty—and chatted animatedly, their voices reverberating throughout the room.

"There's Eloney," Mila whispered loudly.

Their beloved Coolbeensia leader strode up to the oak podium in front of the crowded hall. His warm eyes surveyed the guests.

Everyone quieted down their chatter.

The room grew so silent that the drop of a medallion from Eloney's decorated jacket could be heard.

The president cleared his throat. "Ladies and gentlemen, newly licensed parents, guests, and anyone else I've missed." Eloney had been master of these ceremonies for years, yet as he stood tall and smiled generously, he clearly showed it was like the first time.

"I welcome you to the Coolbeensian Oath of Office Ceremony. Shortly, you will take your Office of Parenthood oaths and be sworn in as professional parents."

The guests glanced at each other, their eyes sparkling.

"Without further ado, let us begin." He shuffled the papers on the podium.

He motioned with his arm. "May I ask all newly licensed parents to please stand."

Mila, Jason, and Vera rose to their feet, along with several others. Mila grabbed her husband's arm and gave it a quick squeeze.

"Please raise your right hand," Eloney instructed, "and recite with me the Coolbeensian oath of the Office of Parenthood."

Mila raised her hand. A mix of hard-earned pride, triumph, and energy rushed through her body.

"I, Eloney Ben Resz—"

She repeated after him, saying, "I, Mila Winston," in place of the president's moniker.

"Do solemnly swear that I accept the uncommon privilege, honor, and responsibility of practicing parenthood in the Republic of Coolbeensia. My actions and decisions henceforth shall be in the best interests of our future children."

She kept her gaze steady, speaking the words of the oath. Though her body stood still, her imagination ran with all the possibilities parenthood would bring: packing school lunches with heart-shaped sandwiches, cheering them on at T-ball, and letting them bring inside the frogs they'd found hopping around the backyard.

"I promise to uphold the Constitution of the Republic of Coolbeensia. In so doing, I will work to parent in accordance with the rule of law, which promotes truth, love, justice, care, equality, peace, and liberty for all."

The room hummed with the chorus of people echoing those beautiful words. A buoyant sensation filled Mila's being. She was finally in the midst of like-minded professionals who'd proven their dedication to the ideals of parenthood. She'd earned her rightful place among them.

"I shall conscientiously and courageously parent with justice and protect the inherent human rights, dignities, and meaningful liberties of our children."

Mila's chin quivered slightly. The president expressed the ideals she'd believed in all her adult life, first as a teacher, then as a parenthood student, and now as a determined, licensed professional.

"I shall do no harm nor shall I manipulate the law."

She nodded.

"I commit to faithfully discharging my parental duties to my children to the best of my natural and learned abilities. In doing so, I give my word that I shall parent with integrity and civility. So help me providence."

Wiping away tears falling down her cheeks, Mila tried to contain her well of emotions.

The room burst into applause.

Mila joined in, bouncing up and down on her toes and smiling ear to ear.

She turned and hugged her husband tightly. Her tears streamed freely, like the plunging waterfalls of Iceland on a summer day. She'd done it. She'd jumped the final hurdle in the long line of taxing legal requirements to prepare her to become a professional parent herself.

Chapter 24

"Not happenin'," Peter yelled upon reading the letter he'd received in the day's mail. No one sent snail mail these days, except the government. He almost didn't open it. But he did, and it left his skin flushed.

He threw the paper on the couch, letting out an ugly snort. The back of his head smacked against the plush cushion as he fixed his gaze on the popcorn ceiling.

"What's the matter?" Amelia set down her knitting and looked over from the recliner. She was halfway finished with a skull cap for Peter II.

"This letter. That's what." He clenched his jaw so tight he thought it'd break. But he didn't care, not at this moment.

"What does it say?" Amelia resumed wrapping the yarn around her thumb and index finger and the needle.

"It's from the Coolbeensia immigration office."

"Oh?"

"We've just been hit with a deportation order."

Amelia dropped the knitting needles. "What for?"

"We're being charged with breaking the law because we're unlicensed parents. Allegedly, since we failed the Parenthood Competency Test this is our punishment." He rolled his eyes and groaned. "According to this Notice to Appear," he muttered, curling his lips, "we have to report to immigration court."

"And stand in front of that ol' judge again?" Amelia cried out.

"Yeah. Judge Eloney's gonna preside at the hearing. We gotta make our case to stay."

He threw his head back, grabbing clumps of his hair. "Grr, this ain't good news."

"Well, I ain't gonna stand up to no judge." Amelia's eyes grew big as saucers.

"You just let me do all the talkin'," he ordered, glaring at his girlfriend. She was capable of only so much, and he wasn't about to leave his future fate in her hands.

He shook himself out of the dread of imagining Amelia in charge of anything. He picked up the letter and examined the rest of the contents.

"It says here we've been admitted to the Republic of Coolbeensia but are removable for the reasons below."

The first half of that sentence sounded good. Being admitted to the micronation had its perks. It was the latter half that troubled him. He glanced lower down the page and began reading out loud.

"The Coolbeensia Department of Childhood Security alleges that you, Peter Losor and Amelia Bord, are unlicensed parents. It is against the Coolbeensia Constitution to reside within the nation's borders as parents without a license to lawfully practice parenthood."

He stared at the paper incredulously for a second and then continued farther down.

"You are ordered—"

Peter stopped and scoffed at the blatant wording. "Ordered? Ha, no one orders Peter Losor around."

"Come on, what else does it say?" Amelia asked, leaning forward.

Grudgingly, Peter continued. "You are ordered to appear before Honorable Judge Eloney of the Coolbeensia Department of Justice at 234 Fleet Street on July 30 at 11:00 a.m. to show why you should not be removed from the Republic of Coolbeensia based on the charges set forth above."

"Crikey." Peter flung the letter again. It coasted to the floor at Amelia's feet.

Peter II started crying from his crib in a corner at the other end of the room.

Amelia picked up her knitting needles and began knitting the next few stitches.

"Our son is crying," Peter told her, as if she didn't hear.

"And?" Amelia replied, purling the next few stitches. She knitted two stitches and then purled two, on and on.

"Don't you wanna give him what he needs?"

Amelia exhaled loudly and dropped the knitting in her lap. "Don't you see I'm busy?"

"Busy?" Peter flung his head back. "Doing what?"

She held up the half-knitted cap and needles with gray yarn wrapped around them. "Can't you see?"

By this time, Peter II started to cry louder.

Peter let out a heavy sigh. "You're telling me knitting is more important than our son?"

Amelia shook her head, as if disappointed by her boyfriend's sheer ignorance. "The virtues of knitting are underestimated. When I get into the flow, which I did a minute before this chaos started, my stress disappears." She glanced down at the string trailing from the ball of yarn and gave it a pull. "Ya know, the rhythm of working the needles is so relaxing." She bared her teeth. "Babies ain't one bit relaxing."

Peter grunted, feeling a knot in his stomach.

"Knitting puts me in a good mood." She started to manipulate the needles faster. "Crying babies just put me in a bad one. Humph!" Upon venting, Amelia returned to her normal knitting rhythm: two knit stiches and then two purl stitches. "Plus, it gives me purpose. See here? I'm knitting a skull cap for it." She pointed to her half-

178

completed gray wool creation. "Don't think I do nothin' for it," she grumbled.

Her boyfriend rolled his eyes again. Amelia had no clue—about anything.

"I'm in control when I knit. Nothin' stops me from my favorite pastime." She tilted her head to one side. "I even find it sorta therapeutic." A little smile escaped her lips.

At this point, Peter II wailed at the top of his lungs.

"Our son has been crying for the past twenty minutes," Peter scolded, his voice escalating, his eyes squinting and his expression tightening.

"Well, do something about it." Amelia didn't even bother to look up. She was at it again, stitch two, then purl two. By golly, she proved she wasn't going to be a mother in the least sense of the word.

Peter leaped off the couch and stomped to the crib. He grabbed a bottle of milk from the dresser and fed his son. The baby took the bottle and drank and drank until he burped.

"He was just hungry, that's all," he said, returning to the couch and plopping down. At least his son wasn't making a fuss anymore. But he had bigger worries looming over his head.

"Well, maybe he'll shush now."

A few minutes of silence passed between them.

"If we don't make our case, where'll we go?" Amelia asked.

"We definitely can't go back to Kansas."

"Or anywhere near it," she added.

"We're fugitives, wanted in all fifty states on insane drug charges. Who knew we'd get caught red-handed? Nothin' will convince me to go back to the US." Peter rubbed his face. "It's way too risky. We'll be on the cops' radar night and day. I'll never sleep a wink. I can't be a good salesman and satisfy my customers when the law keeps interferin' in my business. How am I gonna make a decent livin'?"

"Yeah, it's so unfair." Amelia's eyes grew downcast. "Wh-what about Unibrowumbia?"

"That awful place?" Peter recoiled at merely hearing the name of the most despicable micronation ever to exist on this side of the hemisphere. "What a dump." He made a shooing motion with his hand. "Unibrowumbia don't hold a candle to Coolbeensia."

"A candle? I thought we was talkin' about where we was gonna go."

He rolled his eyes. Poor, helpless, witless Amelia.

"Darlin', I'm talkin' about the good quality of life here in Coolbeensia. We ain't got to worry about no thugs hustling us. Rivals don't exist here. The neighborhoods are peaceful, just how I like it." He sat his portly body back and crossed his arms over his shaggy chest. Random chest hairs poked out from beneath his white cotton-blend tank undershirt.

He was staying put, no matter what.

"Yep, I feel all right here."

"The air is always clean. The food is good." He licked his lips, harkening back to the cheap burek pitas, yuca fries, roasted chicken with a Spanish twist, and the best gyros his taste buds had ever got ahold of for a few brincadors. He and Amelia dined like royalty in Coolbeensia, unlike back in Kansas, where everyday folks paired chili with cinnamon rolls—the most unlikely combo on the planet. He'd never acquired a taste for the dish, no matter how iconic it was.

"Don't forget we live in an apartment with an actual front door, not a rundown shack that ain't got one."

"Heck, even the weather is nicer."

"Yeah," Amelia agreed, gazing wistfully off into the distance. "We ain't gotta stand out in the cold, workin' to make a sale."

Peter tossed out all the good aspects of living in Coolbeensia and the infinite reasons he didn't want to return to Unibrowumbia or any of the fifty US states in his lifetime.

He pursed his lips and knitted his brow. "I'm gonna defend my right to stay, one way or the other."

Chapter 25

July 30 arrived in the blink of an eye. It was National Éclair Day. The schools were closed in observance of this national holiday.

"Hon, on my day off," Mila said, relaxing on the couch, "I'm going shopping. I bought the prenatal vitamins already. Next, I need to browse the shops for baby girl and baby boy onesies." She had a lot to look forward to after earning her professional license.

Jason's eyebrow went up. "Pink *and* blue? How'd you know which one we're going to have?"

"I don't. It's just in case we have a boy or a girl. We'll be ready either way." A good parent stood prepared for whoever popped out. "Besides, I can't wait to start trying to make a baby."

Jason thrust his chest out like a superhero.

Mila began typing a list of the essentials she'd need once their baby arrived. "Car seat, stroller, baby monitor, bassinet . . ." She looked up at her husband. "Do you think a crib or a bassinet?"

"Well, a crib will last longer."

She dropped her head again, typing into the note app on her phone. "Crib is more practical, since a bassinet is good for only a couple months. Oh! A playpen and something to give our future baby a bath. Hmm, maybe a sling seat to fit in the kitchen sink." She added those items to her growing list.

"Honey, we aren't even pregnant yet. Don't you think we should wait until we've actually conceived?" Jason asked, extending the footrest of the recliner.

Mila looked up with a blank expression. She didn't understand her husband's point of view. "Why would we do that? The earlier we start preparing, the better."

She fell back on the couch. Currently, her list was complete, but this was their first time preparing for a baby, and it was easy to overlook essentials.

"Ugh, how could I forget. Diapers!" She flung her arms out. "They'll eat up a huge chunk of our budget. I heard somewhere that babies need almost one hundred per week." She typed it into her notes.

"We really should wait on the diapers. They're pretty pricey. Why don't we just save up for diapers and buy them once we need them—you know, once it's confirmed we're expecting?"

Jason made total sense but not to Mila, who was overcome by the thrill of planning for her first baby. Granted, they hadn't even tried to make a baby yet, with all the legal hurdles they had to jump through. But now that that exhausting period was over, she could relax. And conceiving babies came a thousand times more easily in a state of utter relaxation.

"Ugh, I don't see the point in waiting. We've got financial stability, a place for the baby, and two eager and willing *licensed* parents. Starting a family was the whole reason we moved to Coolbeensia. Why should we delay our dreams?"

Her husband didn't argue. How could he? She knew what she was talking about. She was always the right one, and this discussion was no exception.

"Oh, and today is National Éclair Day. Eclairs are Eloney's second-favorite treat, after black bean brownies." She got up, slipped on her shoes, and tugged her socks up her ankle. "I thought I'd go shopping, stop at the bakery for a box of eclairs, and deliver them to him."

She gave Jason a wink. "He'll love them. Can you believe we're on a first-name basis with the president?"

"It's definitely a first," he replied, still sprawled out on his recliner.

Mila started texting.

A minute later her phone chirped. "It's Margaret. She said Eloney isn't home. He's working at the courthouse. Government offices are open despite it being a national holiday. Hmm."

She tucked her phone into her purse. "Hon, I'll be back in a few hours." Mila turned to her husband, who met her at the door and gave her a quick peck on the cheek. "Then we can start making a baby!" She giggled and rushed out the door.

The baby stores were awash in pastel greens, blues, oranges, and pinks. Teeny-tiny doll-like clothes hung on equally teensy plastic hangers and sat neatly folded on shelves in between stuffed teddy bears.

The store carried onesies in all the cutest styles and colors of the rainbow. She picked out a few yellow ones, blue ones, and pink ones, to cover all her bases. Pushing her cart along, she dropped three packages of newborn diapers into it. The crib and other large items could wait. But she browsed the section of baby cribs to get an idea of what designs were available.

Once she'd had enough shopping for the morning, she loaded up her purchases and headed toward the nearest bakery a mile away. Inhaling the sweet scents of cinnamon and vanilla boosted her mood—not that she needed a pick-me-up, considering she and Jason were on a noble mission of producing a baby. She bought a half-dozen chocolate éclairs, freshly baked at 6:00 a.m., according to the cheerful cashier.

Under the sweltering July sun, condensation appeared on the thick strips of chocolate already. She had a mind to get the éclairs to Eloney before they melted completely. Otherwise, they'd be an utter mess and not worth presenting to her good friend.

Mila's drive took her to the courthouse at 234 Fleet Street. It was a quaint one-story red-brick building, so small that she counted the windows with one glance, two in front and two on each side. The Coolbeensian flag fluttered next to the clock tower emerging from the roof. She entered through the single white door and asked for Judge Eloney.

The bailiff, with buff arms, a wide stance, and looking like he could take down a professional wrestler—or maybe he was one on his off days—stood outside the courtroom.

"Excuse me, but do you know where I can find Judge Eloney?" Mila asked in her politest voice.

"Ma'am, he's in session. But you can go on in if you want. It's open court," he replied. His tone was soft, a complete opposite to how tough he looked.

"Okay, thanks. I'll do that." She gave him a courteous smile and walked inside with the box of éclairs.

She glanced around and took a seat on one of the long wooden benches.

As she got comfortable, her ears picked up a gruff but whiny voice, yet oddly familiar. Her hearing grew acute. She directed her attention to where the voice came from— up front.

Mila squinted to see. Judge Eloney sat on the judge's bench with the Coolbeensia flag to his side. That was expected. He was presiding over the court, after all. He leaned on his clenched fist, as if he was both bored and a little angry.

But another voice, one that made her stomach turn, also reverberated through the court room.

"Yes, my name is Peter Losor."

Mila did a double take. It was Peter, standing there in his jeans and sweater vest. She knew he meant trouble, but what was he doing in court? There was only one way to find out. Leaning forward so as not to miss a word, she gave the case her rapt attention.

Judge Eloney next confirmed Amelia's identity. In an unemotional tone of voice, he began to address procedural problems and summarized the immigration court process.

"Do you need an interpreter?" Judge Eloney asked.

"No, your honor," Peter replied. He leaned toward the mic. "And I will be representing myself."

"A pro se litigant. All right, at your own risk, but you will be held to the standard expected of an attorney," the judge warned him with a stern gaze.

"Understood, your honor."

Mila brought the plastic container of éclairs against her chest. The crushing plastic produced a crinkling sound, which prompted her to set the box on the seat.

Once the formalities were over, the hearing began.

"Mr. Losor, you are neither a citizen nor a national of the Republic of Coolbeensia. The traffic officer who stopped you months ago confirmed you and your girlfriend, Ms. Bord, provided him with fake IDs," Judge Eloney stated. His face expressed a grimness that Mila had never seen on him before.

"You are a native of the United States and a citizen of the United States."

Mila gasped but quickly brought her hand to her mouth. Peter was not a natural-born citizen of Coolbeensia? That partially explained his grossly dismissive attitude toward its laws.

"You entered the Republic of Coolbeensia unlawfully. But that's not why we're here today." The judge looked sternly at Peter and Amelia and breathed in deeply, almost as if hopelessly.

"You remained in Coolbeensia after becoming parents and failing to pass the Parenthood Competency Test. As a result of being unlicensed parents, you are being charged with unlawful conduct. Do you understand the charges?"

Peter lowered his head. "Yes, your honor."

Her disruptive former classmate acted more humbly than she'd ever seen.

"On the basis of the preceding, it is charged that you are subject to removal from the Republic of Coolbeensia in pursuant to the following provision of Coolbeensian law."

Judge Eloney shuffled a few papers on the bench and began reading.

"Section 123(a)(4)(B) of the Constitution, after entering Coolbeensia, you have remained here and bore a child without earning a license to practice parenthood. This is in violation of Coolbeensian law."

Peter was already a father? In Coolbeensia? How did he avert the law for so long? Mila inched to the edge of her seat. This case produced more juicy news than a television soap opera.

"You will be removed from Coolbeensia and deported to the United States, your country of origin."

Peter gazed straight ahead, neither flinching nor blinking.

"You have the right to appeal the decision. Do you waive or reserve your right to appeal?"

"I reserve my right to appeal," Peter answered.

"Your appeal rights are reserved. You will be sent a written notice of your next hearing."

Judge Eloney rested both his arms on the raised bench. "Mr. Losor, in my more than two decades of presiding over the court, you are the first to fight my decision. Coolbeensia's foundation is its laws. You broke the most important one, the one that defines our micronation, allows it to thrive, and ensures the happiness of our most vulnerable citizens. Due to the unprecedented nature of this matter, there is no doubt in my mind that this case will become a high-profile one." The judge pounded his gavel. "See you in court."

His head hung low, Peter moseyed from the counsel table with Amelia trailing behind.

Mila jumped up and ran out of the courtroom. Once she reached the parking lot, she realized she still had the box of chocolate éclairs in her hand. She grimaced and returned to the courtroom.

She handed Judge Eloney the treats with the chocolate still holding firm. She itched to start a heart-to-heart conversation about what just unfolded in court. But she knew better than to inquire about this highly concerning matter with a sitting judge. Her opinions could influence his judicial conduct, and she valued his fairness in all circumstances. So, she mumbled a few niceties and raced back home.

Jason greeted her with a big smile and open arms. "Honey, you're back! Ready to go make a baby?"

"Not now, Jason." A scowl crossed Mila's face.

"What's the matter?"

"Peter, that's what."

"What'd he do now? I thought that chapter was over."

"He was at court. He intends to appeal the judge's decision to deport him for not having a license to practice parenthood." Mila choked up as she spoke. "Did you know he was a parent already?"

"So—so, you're not interested in making a baby?"

"No!" she screamed. "Not now, not while this case is going on. It's too distracting." She rubbed her forehead. "The outcome of this case could set a very bad legal precedent."

Her husband scratched his head.

Staring wildly into Jason's eyes, she grabbed him by the arms. "Don't you get it? This case is going to be huge, probably Coolbeensia's most significant. I've got to be there. Every day that Peter shows up in court, I'll be sitting on the benches, lapping up every word."

"That's ludicrous."

"No, it's not. If Peter wins this case, it could change the very reason we came here."

Chapter 26

Mila arrived at the courthouse twenty minutes early for Peter's merit hearing. In the parking lot, she noticed bumper stickers glorifying the north, east, west, and southern parts of Coolbeensia. Naturally, each had its unique culture, but the nation's most humanitarian law—the one Peter was fighting today—united them all. Citizens had driven from all around the nation to witness this trailblazing case.

She hopped up the steps, opening the door to throngs of women and men, young and old, single people and couples, packing the courthouse. She could barely squeeze through the hall. She knew this case would draw national attention, but she never expected this vast multitude of spectators. Judge Eloney was right—this case did turn out to be high-profile. And why wouldn't it have been? Peter was about to challenge the very law that made Coolbeensia the nation with the highest quality of life on Earth.

Mila climbed over knobby knees and bulky purses resting on laps before she found a seat in the gallery. She could barely breathe with people sitting closely on either side of her. Relief came quickly.

"All rise," the bailiff, looking buff as ever, instructed the spectators in the courtroom. Everyone, including Mila, stood on their feet. She had a breath of air, instead of being squished like sardines in the gallery.

Judge Eloney, dressed in a long, flowing blue robe printed with tiny smiling brown beans, stepped up to the judge's bench. Earlier, when she'd dropped off the éclairs, they'd chatted about how Margaret had sewn him his robe. He'd said he rarely needed to wear it, because most Coolbeensians were law abiding.

"You may be seated," the bailiff said. "Court is now in session." He took his position against the side wall.

Mila sat more ready than ever to hear Peter make his case for why he had the right to stay in Coolbeensia, despite his egregious violation of the law. Ha! No one was above the law, certainly not a law that held such gravity. He'd have a hard time arguing his defense, considering the strict licensure mandate required of all parents, regardless of class or creed.

She rested her chin in her hand and leaned forward.

The biggest case in the history of the micronation was called.

"We now call *Losor vs. Coolbeensia*."

Peter ambled up to the table like a drunkard who'd chugged too many beers.

Once he took his position, the bailiff asked Peter to hold his right hand up. "Do you swear by providence to tell the truth, the whole truth, and nothing but the truth?"

"I truly declare I'll tell the whole truth and nothing but the truth."

The bailiff returned to his post, and the hearing began.

Judge Eloney started by asking Peter for his direct testimony. "Mr. Losor, please tell the court why you left your home country."

Entranced, Mila didn't blink.

"Your honor," Peter started, "due to the nature of my entrepreneurial business, I was forced to leave the United States. I can't return for the same reason."

The judge's face seemed relaxed, with the lines softening. He'd clearly accepted Peter's excuse. But Mila didn't. What exactly did his entrepreneurial business involve? He did mention sales and marketing once before. She tilted her head. She couldn't get a straight answer off his testimony.

"Mr. Losor, per your earlier hearing, you were made aware of the charges against you. Let me repeat them. You are charged with violating the Coolbeensia Constitution, specifically, having a child without earning the mandated parental license. You, sir, are unlawfully practicing parenthood."

"I understand, Your Honor," Peter replied with a nod.

"Well, then, please state your case as to why you, as a father, should stay in Coolbeensia without a license to practice." Judge Eloney sat back and crossed his arms, as if waiting for the most idiotic defense he'd ever heard.

Peter leaned his round head of messy hair toward the mic. "Your honor, I defend my right to stay in Coolbeensia without a parental license."

The judge didn't move a muscle. Clearly, he wasn't impressed.

"I don't need no license to have my son because it's my inalienable right to have a child."

The spectators in the courtroom began to murmur.

Judge Eloney leaned forward, giving Peter an incredulous stare.

"It's my fundamental right to procreate, and the laws of Coolbeensia ain't got no right to deprive me of it. Fatherhood is a common law right. As a human being, I'm entitled to that right, plus the right to life, the right to freedom, and the right to the pursuit of happiness."

He leaned into the mic again and spoke in a low but firm tone. "You Honor, my right to be a parent is independent of the government of Coolbeensia."

The courtroom exploded in loud whispering as people voiced confusion.

"Order in the court! Order in the court!" the bailiff shouted.

Judge Eloney flinched.

A feeling of paralysis overcame Mila's limbs. Her thoughts went blank. Her brain might've momentarily stopped working, but clearly Peter's hadn't. She did a double take. The sloppy posture, the portly body, the raggedy sweater vest, the faded jeans. Yep, it was Peter Losor up there uttering those powerful words.

Furrowing his brow, Judge Eloney made strong eye contact with Peter.

"Mr. Losor, it is not your right to procreate that's at stake but to have a child without a license and rear that child in everyday Coolbeensian society. The risk of bringing up a child without adequate skill and care is higher in unlicensed parents."

Mila wanted to give the judge a pat on the back. He'd made a vital point. Just like unlicensed drivers were responsible for nearly one-quarter of fatal accidents, unlicensed parents were more likely to fall into habits of neglect or worse. She shivered at the thought.

She continued to pay heed as the judge spoke in a steady, low pitch.

"A child who is neglected or maltreated has a greater chance of experiencing dire consequences in adulthood, ranging from drug or alcohol abuse to breaking the law. They can grow up to be destructive not only to themselves but to others. Therefore, your unlawful actions pose a public safety risk."

Definitely. Child-rearing was playing the long game. It wasn't a raise-'em-quick scheme after which parents could wipe their hands clean. They needed to prepare eighteen years into the future.

The judge wasn't finished.

"In the public interest of our micronation, uniform regulations are necessary to preserve safety and order. As a result, parental licensing mandates are critical."

Mila nodded as the tension left her face. Even with skillful and careful parenting, children were vulnerable to running into trouble. Licensed parents trained for the unforeseeable and possessed the skill to manage and mitigate risks. Enforcing well-thought-out regulations, starting with the parents, helped preserve harmony across all of Coolbeensian society. As far as she could see, it had worked. Coolbeensia took the number one spot for the happiest nation on Earth.

"I disagree, Your Honor," Peter argued, his nostrils flaring. "My right to be a part of the Coolbeensian population necessitates my right to contribute to the Coolbeensian population. By reproducing, I fulfill my natural right."

The courtroom burst into chaos as spectators grimaced, ran their hands through their hair, and asked each other in no indirect terms if they'd heard what they'd just heard.

The bailiff again quieted down the court.

In the silence of the room, where a pin drop could be heard, Judge Eloney made his counterargument.

"Mr. Losor, I am aware of an individual's right to procreate. However, that individual does not have the right to bear a child without a license here in Coolbeensia, as licensure serves a valid public purpose. Regulating parenthood is vital to securing a child's health, happiness, and overall welfare—which in turn secures the health, happiness, and overall welfare of the Coolbeensian adults they grow up to be."

Peter's face flushed beet red. Beads of sweat ran down his temples. He looked like he was about to explode.

Mila sat still as a statue. Her only movement was her biting her nails in sheer anticipation.

"Your Honor, a parental license basically asks that I get permission for having my son." Peter crossed his arms over his chest. He drew himself up to his full height. He stared at Judge Eloney, as if challenging him like an angry bull challenges the flashy matador in the ring. His voice as rough as sandpaper, he muttered in an unsettling tone, "Peter Losor don't ask permission from nobody."

Chapter 27

Mila twirled the noodles with her fork and pushed the flaky fish back and forth across her plate. She washed the dinnerware with the lemony-yellow sauce. As she rested her chin on her hand, her thoughts went elsewhere than on her sumptuous dinner.

"Uh, honey? You not hungry? You usually love my baked fish paired with lemon cream sauce." Jason shoved a forkful of noodles into his mouth as he kept his eyes on her.

"Oh, I don't know. This case. Peter's case. It's bothering me." She laid down her fork.

"What for? You know how it'll end. Judge Eloney will staunchly guard the Constitution. He'll strike down Peter's unconstitutional actions. Coolbeensia law won't change. Once the distractions are all over, we can start our family just like we planned."

Mila leaned against her lattice-back dining chair and let out a long sigh. "I'm not so sure. Judge Eloney is responsible for interpreting Coolbeensian law. Eloney is fair—too fair, I worry." She pushed her shiny brunette hair behind her ear and kept her gaze down.

"He's got both integrity and a deep well of compassion. Peter's argument has been surprisingly lucid so far. I jumped at least ten times through the merit hearing at things he said. Obviously, the spectators in the court were moved too."

She glanced up at Jason with her neatly trimmed brows knitted.

"If Peter's arguments change their minds, Eloney might be swayed by them, feeling the pressure of the general public. And we know how influential the court of public opinion is."

She'd covered the dark circles under eyes with concealer. Still, she could feel her husband's gaze detecting her fatigue—a tiredness that came from tossing and turning all night worrying about the outcome of the case.

"You've got to remember, Eloney, as the executive and legislative branch, designed this very important law himself. And for good reason. He wouldn't change his mind so easily. His whole ideology rests on it."

He shoved another forkful of baked fish into his mouth after dousing it in the sauce.

Mila sighed, her gaze still directed downward. "Yeah, but societies change, evolve. Maybe what was working then might not work now."

"You have little faith in Eloney, don't you?"

She bolted upright at the mere suggestion and looked her husband in the eyes, the first time during that evening's dinner. "No, I do! I have lots of faith in our dear friend. It's just that it's not possible to find a judge who's completely impervious. I'd love to believe Eloney can leave all the dangerous influences out of the courtroom. But in the end, he's a human being."

She slouched again in her chair.

Jason remained silent. It was clear he couldn't counter her rationality.

Mila pinched at the skin of her throat. "In the next few hearings, if Peter makes his case that his human rights are being violated, it could affect Eloney's decision." She spoke in a quieter tone. "It might bring an amendment to the Constitution. Then—"

She choked up, as if her throat suddenly grew constricted.

Jason reached across the table and stroked her hand.

"Then Coolbeensia will become just like Illinois, or Florida, or Minnesota, or any one of the other fifty states, where unfortunate kids are vulnerable to the worst of the worst."

Her voice grew increasingly louder, defiant. "As a teacher, as a future parent, and as a human being, I can't live like that. Not after joyfully living my ideals to the fullest here in Coolbeensia. Being in this one-of-a-kind micronation has opened my eyes to the possibilities, the potential for happiness and security for myself and my future kids—and I can't return to living in conditions of unbridled chaos."

Jason offered his thoughtful expression.

Mila got up with effort as if she struggled with the world resting on her petite shoulders. She absentmindedly scraped her dinner into a glass container and shoved it into the back of the fridge.

Her husband seemed to fumble for the right words. He yelled out, "You really should've eaten a little more, hon." Without looking back, she trudged to the living room with her head hung low.

Her face pale, she opened her laptop and began typing away. Submitting her lengthy application to the Coolbeensia Professional Parent Guild would take her mind off the case, at least for a few hours.

"Petey." Amelia's voice sounded whiny. What could she possibly want now? Peter turned from the computer. He'd been busy preparing for his upcoming court appearance.

He'd outlined the subject of his next defense, which he anticipated he'd argue heatedly with the judge in a month.

"Yeah."

"That hearing of ours. I can't take it." She wrung her hands as if she were wringing wet laundry. Of course, a dryer was included in the apartment. It was one of those high-tech models. The problem was that Amelia couldn't figure out the controls. She dried their clothes the old-fashioned way. Amelia could be depended on for only so many things.

"What d'you mean you can't take it?"

"It's full of arguments." Amelia wrinkled her nose. "I don't like arguments. I feel sorta threatened." She made herself small, like she didn't want to be seen, and kept fidgeting her hands.

Peter winced. An uncomfortable lump grew in his throat. "It's just a hearing. That's how they go. I argue and the judge argues back. Fair and square."

She murmured something inaudible.

With a quick snort, he pointed to her. "Now you listen here. You'd better prepare, 'cause it's gonna be like this for the next few hearings."

Amelia shifted in the recliner as if she'd sat on the flat end of a USB cable and attempted to reduce her discomfort.

"Then I don't wanna go."

"To court?" His eyes popped.

"Yeah."

"Listen, we're in this together. If the judge wins, we'll both be deported. Do you want that?" he asked, scrunching his face. "I'm tryin' to fight for us so we can stay."

"But all the arguments, the extra money we got to fork over for the babysitter. I'm feelin' it, and it ain't pretty. I don't want no more of all that." Amelia shrugged her shoulders, as if she failed to grasp the seriousness of their predicament.

Peter tried to regain his calm. "Then what're you gonna do?"

Amelia closed her eyes and sat quietly on the recliner for a minute. A small smile appeared at the corners of her thin lips.

"I'll volunteer to leave."

"Coolbeensia?"

"Yeah."

"But where'll you go?"

"Oh, I dunno. Maybe Unibrowumbia?"

"You hate that place!"

"But I hate arguments more," she shouted back, growing red in the face.

"All right, all right." Peter pushed his hands in front of his body. "We'll figure somethin' out." He scratched his head. "Maybe you can stay at Fred's old house for a while, until the case winds down. He ain't stayin' there no more, and you'll be fine."

"Good." She perked up. "Then when you're done arguing, I'll come back." She gave him a big smile. "So, what d'you want for dinner? We got macaroni, red beans and rice . . ."

Peter tuned her out.

He sat staring vacantly as his girlfriend continued to yap. He had to notify the judge of Amelia's decision.

Once she got up and walked into the kitchen, still rolling dinner menu items off her tongue, Peter shook himself out of what had just happened. His girlfriend was leaving him alone on the chopping block. Figured. She couldn't be depended on for most things. She'd take Peter II with her too. Knowing her maternal capabilities firsthand, his son's welfare was another concern.

He rubbed his eyes. None of this could be real.

But it was as real as daylight. He shook his jowls. His court hearing was coming up, and he had to prepare.

Feeling like a ton of bricks rested on his stocky chest, he slowly turned to the computer screen. He'd have to inform the judge at the next hearing that his girlfriend requested a voluntary departure. From what he'd gathered about Coolbeensian law, she'd avoid the deportation order and its record on her immigration file.

Funny thing. It turned out he'd learned more about Coolbeensian laws while preparing to defend his right to stay than in his nine months at the Parenthood Polytechnic. Eh, he shrugged it off. He now had real reasons to need to learn the law.

He returned to study the rules surrounding Amelia's voluntary departure. She had the means to leave Coolbeensia, which satisfied the first requirement. The second requirement left him rubbing his chin. How was he going to prove that she'd been a good person for at least three years?

Chapter 28

On the morning of Peter's second hearing, Mila arrived at the courthouse at 9:30 a.m. sharp.

The courtroom was more jam-packed than on the first day of the hearing. People stood shoulder to shoulder against the walls and sat sandwiched together in the gallery.

Mila could barely breathe as she inched her way through the tightly packed crowd. The one-room courthouse was barely equipped to handle high-profile cases. But, as Eloney had said, he rarely had a need to preside over hearings because Coolbeensian citizens were usually upright.

She didn't even look for a few inches of open space into which she could wiggle herself. Rather, she found a spot standing next to the bailiff, looking as buff as ever. His bald head gleamed under the ceiling light. He reminded her of the English queen's royal guard, with a stiff upper lip, but without all the pomp and circumstance. She glanced up at his six-foot-two frame and gave a demure smile.

He simply stared straight ahead, immovable and proud, like the Sierra Nevada's Mount Whitney.

As ten o'clock approached, the courtroom grew abuzz with the hums and drones of spectators talking. She heard whisperings about how the ruling of this case would determine if they fled the micronation or stayed. Mila closed her eyes. She could relate.

The nonstop bustling of spectators inside the courtroom gave off the steady sounds of a rainforest alive with insects rubbing their legs, monkeys chattering, and hummingbirds flapping their wings on a sultry morning—the perfectly distracting conditions to lure a stealthy tiger on the prowl for a satisfying meal.

Mila shook herself to rid her mind of the vivid comparison. Peter was this very tiger on the hunt to chew up and spit out Coolbeensian law. But he wouldn't, no matter how strong his case was. No, he couldn't, not in a million gazillion years. She felt compelled to reassure herself.

At exactly ten o'clock, the bailiff instructed the spectators to rise. Judge Eloney sauntered up to the bench, looking too weary for another pointless round in the ring. The typical procedures took place, and the hearing began.

Judge Eloney, with an unapologetic frown on his face, seemed as if he didn't want to argue with a fool like the one standing before him.

Peter started to inform the judge that Amelia requested a volunteer departure. "And I can prove she's been a good—"

The judge banged his wooden gavel before Peter could say another word. "Granted."

Speechless, Peter stared at the judge.

Mila jerked her head back. Judge Eloney didn't even wait to hear him give a reason. He must've really wanted her gone stat.

"Now, let's move on."

Peter bowed his head. "Yes, Your Honor." He dared to appear before judge in yet another threadbare sweater vest and jeans, faded as if they'd spent too much time in the sun. He probably didn't even own a pair of slacks and a collared dress shirt. If he did own a tie, he wasn't the type of man who knew how to fasten it. He wore a look that would surely foretell his downfall.

Judge Eloney leaned forward with his arms resting in a pretzel shape on the glossy bench. "Mr. Losor, we've been discussing rights all along, the right of the parent to do this and do that. Blah, blah, blah."

His eyes narrowed, nearly squinting.

"But the only legitimate right here is the child's right to competent parents who work hard to earn their licensure and prove they are fit for the demanding job—a job that's almost guaranteed to last for years."

The courtroom erupted in applause, whistles, and hoots. It was clear whose side the people were on.

"Order in the court," the bailiff shouted. "Order in the court!" His powerful yells put all the spectators back in their seats immediately. Mila covered her ears, since she stood right next to him.

Judge Eloney appeared visibly indifferent to the spontaneous show of support. "Earning a license is a privilege that constitutes an agreement between the parent and Coolbeensia, whereby the former vows they shall parent in good faith."

Peter cleared his throat and leaned into the mic. "I disagree, Your Honor."

Eloney's brow arched. "Oh? How so?"

He rested an index finger on his cheek and listened with his other arm across his chest.

"Your Honor, havin' a son with no license ain't nothin' but my right—it ain't no privilege." He stepped back, as if he thought the judge would be too speechless to counterargue.

Murmurs filled the courtroom as people whispered to each other.

Mila brought her fingers to her lips. The foundation of Peter's argument today lay on the clear difference between a right and a privilege. Humph, he forgot he was in Coolbeensia, where things didn't work like the rest of the uproarious world. Her pulse racing, she watched the drama unfold.

"Mr. Losor, remember where you are. You're not in some free-for-all country where parents do whatever they want at the expense of their own children. You are in Coolbeensia, where we consider it a privilege to be a parent, and not a right. You must earn this privilege." He paused. "Licensure itself is a privilege."

Peter shook his head, his cheeks flapping like Jell-O. "No, no, it ain't. It's a right."

Judge Eloney threw his hands up. "How is a parental license not a right when it can be legally denied? You, sir, should know. By failing the PCT, you've been denied the privilege of licensure."

"Your Honor, the exam was rigged. I know it. I would've passed if it weren't for—"

"Mr. Losor," the judge scolded. "I've had enough of your excuses. We are not here to debate your scores."

"No, you don't get it. Part of that exam was in Greek!"

Judge Eloney pounded his gavel. "I said no more ridiculous outbursts from you, or I'll hold you in contempt of court."

"No, but—"

"That's it, Mr. Losor. You are in contempt of court and are fined one hundred brincadors."

Peter shut up quickly.

"Ugh, fine, Your Honor." He hung his head.

"Now we'll proceed if you can do so civilly."

Peter nodded.

"Okay, let us continue."

"Judge," Peter pleaded, "I got the right to be a father with no license as much as I got the right to free speech with no license." Peter sounded almost desperate.

The judge glowered at him. "Let me define what a right and a privilege are, Mr. Losor, as you seem to fail to understand. A privilege is given once it is earned, but it can be taken away. A right, on the other hand, cannot be denied or taken away. To be a parent is an opportunity reserved for the skilled and dedicated. As a result, this privilege is not available to everyone, at least not here."

"Peter, my hero! I love you, Peter!"

Mila whipped her head to the side to see a young woman in a purple leather miniskirt with green streaks in her hair reaching out for him with both arms from the back of the gallery.

Peter, too, spun his head around, with a big smile plastered on his face and his stocky chest pushed out.

The bailiff rushed to contain the commotion, carrying the screaming lady over his shoulder and out of the courtroom.

He reentered moments later to a disrupted courtroom. With a calm demeanor, he again returned order. Mila simply looked up at him with awe. This burly bailiff performed his job perfectly.

Scratching his jaw slowly, Judge Eloney seemed baffled. He let out a long exhale, collected himself, and then resumed his argument in favor of Coolbeensia.

"Mr. Losor, flattered as you may be by this disruptive fan of yours, if you do not put forth the effort to earn a parental license, you are not entitled to the special privilege. As you know, not everyone is willing to spend the time, energy, and dedication needed to obtain a professional license to practice.

"Even when an individual enjoys the privilege to hold a parental license, they are not free to do whatever they please. Licensed parents are held to high standards and are expected to abide by the rules of the profession, such as refraining from behaviors that would threaten the well-being of their dependents."

Peter glanced to his right, where Amelia sat quietly with her head down, not looking at anyone.

"High standards are necessary in the field of professional parenting, in part because the parents' actions impact the wider community and the micronation.

"Parents wield a certain level of influence. Licensed or not, they have the power to affect others—not only their own children but society.

"A system of checks must be in place to ensure that only qualified individuals hold this position of power. Coolbeensian law holds parents accountable. And if they fail, they shall live with the repercussions."

Mila glanced around the room. Did anyone else wonder what those repercussions were? Did licensed parents ever lose their credentials? She made a mental note to find out later.

"Mr. Losor, per Coolbeensian law, the privilege of parenthood can be taken away if violations occur. It is not an inherent right, as you claim, since by definition, rights cannot be taken away."

Judge Eloney sat back and crossed his arms.

Peter, with a blank expression on his face, spoke into the mic. "I'm a parent, and I don't need to do no work to earn it. I never did, and here I am, a father. So, see? It proves it's my right."

The judge tilted his head and stayed silent.

"It's like free speech. I ain't gotta do nothin' to speak freely. It don't cost no one else if I speak freely. Just the same, I don't need no parent license, since it don't cost no one else nothin'."

"Again, you fail to grasp the meaning behind the law. It does in fact cost others when a child is neglected. It costs society, and it costs the well-being of the child.

"You are not free to pursue an occupation without first obtaining the mandatory license."

"Oh, oh, on the contrary, Your Honor," Peter argued, pushing his hands in front of him. "My right to parent without a license is a form of expression."

Judge Eloney rolled his eyes.

"If you are not qualified to hold a professional license, or if you violate the parenting laws of our micronation, your privileges to the role are denied. Isn't that why you're here today, Mr. Losor?"

Peter gulped.

Chapter 29

"You look cheery!" Jason exclaimed as he walked through the front door. The sun took a gentle dive below the horizon. He'd just finished up the workday at the school.

Mila met him in the hall, sending one leg up behind her as she stretched her neck to give him a kiss.

"It's impossible. You couldn't have gone to the hearing this morning. You're too cheerful, sparkling like champagne." Jason set down his leather briefcase and undid the first two buttons of his dress shirt.

"Ah," she said, "the tables have turned."

"Oh, really? Wait a minute. First off, your school finally found a sub?"

Mila's shoulder slumped. "Ugh, that was the worst part. I was itching for them to call me. But almost every substitute teacher was at the courthouse for the biggest trial of Coolbeensian history. Finding someone took a lot of calls."

She clapped her hands. "But they found one! And, yes, I was at the court."

"How'd it go?" Jason asked, making his way into the apartment.

She followed behind him, clasping her hands to her chest. "Peter's heading downhill. He's losing confidence. Everything about his latest defense is getting weaker."

Jason removed his dress socks, one foot at a time, and plopped on the couch. "Is that the reason you're so happy?"

Her husband's lightheartedness was one of many reasons that drew her to him. He was the perfect foil to her idiosyncratic need for things to be done right. Isn't it what anyone wanted?

"Uh, where do I start?" Mila placed the back of her hand across her forehead. "Peter's arguments no longer hold water. I can feel it like a stick poking me in the hip—he's caving under the pressure, trying to convince the judge he has the right to stay without a license."

She spoke so fast as she paced the living room that she could hardly get the words out without sounding like a motor speedway. "He's confused about the difference between a right and a privilege. He had no idea. Judge Eloney set him straight really fast."

Feeling weightless, she wanted to leap ten feet in the air.

"It looks like Peter will lose in the end." Jason chuckled. "I told you so."

Mila pressed her index finger against her lips. "I just have one burning question. The Parenthood Polytechnic didn't cover it, and I know only one person who'd have the answer."

"What's this burning question? When are we going to make a baby?" Peter joked.

Mila rolled her eyes.

"No, Mr. Smarty Pants." She ran her fingers through her hair. "It's probably rare in Coolbeensia. But what happens when a licensed parent fails to live up to the standards of the profession? I mean, we're all human, and things can shift in the blink of an eye. Parents can get sick and their personalities change, or parenting skills might deteriorate because of their poor condition."

"That's a good question." Jason clasped his hands behind his head and propped his legs on the ottoman. "How're you going to find out?"

"I thought I'd invite Eloney for tea at the Main Street Café. I'm not planning to try to influence his decision on the case at all." She gave her husband a "no way, I'd never stoop so low" look. "That wouldn't be permitted in any jurisdiction on Earth. Could you imagine if it were allowed? It'd be turmoil." She paused to contemplate the scenario and then shook her head. "No, I just want to pick his brain."

She glanced at the blue digits of the clock on the living room side table. "In fact, I ought to head out right now to make it there on time."

Mila had a quick glance in the mirror, smoothed out her hair, grabbed her keys, and rushed out the door.

Eloney sat in the café with a tablet in his hands. It was a cozy place, its white walls splattered with colorful paint, from vibrant red splashes to yellow dots and green swaths—Jackson Pollock style. Abstract art hung on the walls, and modern lamps illuminated the space. The French doors were painted an uncommon pastel green that gave the entire café a lovely country flair.

He swung one leg over the other as Mila approached.

"Eloney! It's good to see you outside of the courtroom in plain clothes. Not that your judicial robe with the little bean print is quirky or anything," she said, greeting him with a smile. "On the other hand, it suits you just fine."

He looked up with a warm smile, his bushy eyebrows raised, and pointed to his tablet. "See, here? The hearing is making the news headlines."

"Just like you predicted." Mila took a seat and set her purse on an empty chair. "The outcome could set a legal precedent and change the very reason Coolbeensian citizens raise their families here."

She picked up the laminated menu. "What'll you have? Tea is on me today."

"Oh, I'll have whatever's hot."

"All right. I'll order for both of us." She perused the assortments of teas: chai, Oolong, rooibos, and green. "Mm. The lavender tea sounds delightful. It's perfect for stress reduction. Just what we need."

She glanced up at her friend, pressing her fingers against her lips. "I mean what *you* need. I'm not stressed at all about the case. In fact—"

In the nick of time, Mila remembered she wasn't there to discuss the case. She closed her mouth.

"Shall we order?" she said with a smile.

Eloney's face radiated a gentle, steady warmth, as if not much irked him. He didn't show a hint of irritation at her near blunder. If any of the other few customers in the café overheard and suspected she was trying to influence the judge, there'd be trouble.

The waiter, in his black apron and oxford shirt, couldn't have arrived soon enough. He took her order.

"Two cups of lavender tea, please."

Shortly after, she lifted her nose to inhale the aromatic scents of the lavender tea: woody, sweet, and with hints of rose. The waiter set down two cups of the piping hot floral tea.

Mila raised her bone China cup embellished with little blue flowers and said, "To our health."

Eloney raised his cup and took a sip. "Mm. That's good."

The hot tea dripping down her throat relaxed her. It instantly transported her to a floral garden blooming with rows upon rows of flourishing lavender shrubs on a sunny day.

She set her teacup down. She'd gone there on a mission, and she was about to fulfill it. After all, she had to plan for potential obstacles to her goal of starting a family there in Coolbeensia.

"Eloney, I've got a sixty-four-thousand-brincador question."

"I'm all ears." He bent his head and took a long sip of tea, which produced splattering sounds.

"Coolbeensian parents are held to very high professional standards. And I'm sure most of them remain honorable and ethical and dedicated to the ideals of their profession."

Mila leaned across the square oak table. "But what happens when a licensed parent errs? I mean, even generally good drivers who hold valid licenses get ticketed all the time. They might make innocent mistakes or go slightly over the speed limit or whatnot."

She rambled on—she had a point to make.

"Lawyers, too, goof up, no matter how long they've been practicing or how hard they try. Like licensed parents here in Coolbeensia, most legal mistakes don't end up in lively malpractice claims."

Eloney simply nodded, listening to her every word with the patience of an old sage.

"No one's perfect. But professionals, whether legal or parental, are expected to perform at a certain level of competency." Mila resorted to a loud whisper. "But what if they slip up?"

Eloney sat quiet for a minute, likely processing the gravity of her question.

Mila wrapped her fingers tightly around the hot teacup. She stared at him, waiting for his answer as her knees bounced under the table.

Her friend took a deep breath as if he were an elite university lecturer preparing to deliver the wisdom of the century. She was his starry-eyed student, aching to fill her empty reservoir with knowledge.

"Let's start by talking about parents and expectant parents without a license or permit. When caught, they are mandated by the courts to take the steps necessary to obtain a license. After failed attempts, they are fined. The brincadors collected fund the provisions at the Center for the Preservation of Happiness and Silliness, where children grow on a personal, social, intellectual, and emotional level."

What an excellent way to utilize financial resources. Mila leaned forward, a puppy dog lapping up the wisdom brimming in a silvery vessel. Eloney knew how to run a courtroom—and a country.

"Now, in cases of serious offenders who continue to raise their children here without a parental license and make no deliberate effort to earn it, they are either deported or jailed for nine months."

"Jailed?" Her eyes popped open.

"Yes, jailed. During this time, remote classes at the Parenthood Polytechnic are available to them for free. The school has always been free to interested students."

Indeed, keeping the school free encouraged hopeful parents of all backgrounds and diversified the parenthood pool.

"The child of the unlicensed parent is boarded at the Center for the Preservation of Happiness and Silliness until the jail sentence is served."

"Ooh. Who takes care of the kids in the center?"

"Well, caregivers hold valid parental licenses and nurture the children with great care and attention. The staff are obligated to take continuing education classes to ensure they stay up to date on the evolving nature of the parenthood profession."

He circled his finger around the rim of the teacup.

Then he looked directly into Mila's glowing face. "As all licensed parents, you, too, are required to take continuing education courses to keep up with the times. Society changes fast, especially with the influx of new technologies. Like any job, parenthood is affected too."

She leaned back and smiled with satisfaction. She wanted to tell every well-meaning parent to raise their families here, the most proficient, family-friendly nation she'd ever encountered.

Eloney grew unnaturally quiet, a drastic change from a second before.

Once he resumed speaking, his voice trembled.

"But when licensed Coolbeensian parents engage in behaviors that endanger their children—"

He teared up, his gray eyes flooding with sorrow.

"Here." Mila grabbed a napkin and handed it to him.

Eloney wiped his tears. "For egregious offenses, such as intentional acts of abuse or neglect, their parental license is revoked. Then, if the misbehaving parent is an immigrant, the individual is deported. Or if a Coolbeensian citizen, they are immediately expelled from the micronation."

Mila blinked rapidly, in full agreement with the strict punishment. "What happens to the child?"

"Well, the child grows up in the center, where they are raised and nurtured by the licensed caregivers I just mentioned until they are of age to properly care for themselves. We have only a small number of kids in the center, but they are well-integrated into the community and live joyfully and carefree."

The tension from Mila's body vanished. "That's a relief."

"All of this comes with due process, of course. The offending parents are given an opportunity to defend themselves in court, as you know firsthand. Folks from all over have been attending the hearings without fail."

Mila nodded, taking a long sip of her soothing tea.

"Based on meticulously kept court records, it's rare for a licensed parent to misbehave after dedicating enormous time and effort to earn a license." He made a flipping motion with his hand. "Sometimes misfortunes do occur. It's just the way the world is."

Eloney's eyes grew downcast upon speaking of the harshness of reality.

"But we try, here in Coolbeensia, to reduce those risks as much as we can. And by golly, it works!"

As he ended his satisfactory explanation with a smile, warm as the lavender tea left at the bottom of her cup, the urge welled up inside Mila to probe into Peter's case. Her opinions and value judgements were on the tip of her tongue, eager to be expressed. But it wasn't in anyone's best interests to hold discussions with a sitting judge presiding over the most significant case in Coolbeensian history.

Chapter 30

The beat-up Chevy chugged toward the border, making grinding and hissing noises. Peter decided to go by the way he first entered Coolbeensia, via the open sections of the border. The obscure route meant the border officials wouldn't hassle him about still not having a valid ID.

"Now you sure you got everything?" Peter asked. "I don't wanna keep havin' to go back and forth."

Amelia nodded. "I'm sure. All my clothes, some cans of food, and my toothbrush." She looked at her boyfriend, twisting her hands. "But I'll only be gone a little while. You'll win this case, right? Then I'll come back. And there ain't gonna be no more arguing."

"That's the plan. This case will wrap up soon in my favor. You'll return from your voluntary departure, then we'll get our lives and career back. We'll start fresh here in Coolbeensia."

"And restart our old ways!"

"Yep," Peter agreed. "Just in a brand-new place."

Amelia giggled as her eyes brightened. "I do miss stayin' in touch with customers, even though the cheap ones just want a teensy ounce. The good ones want a whole brick! Ooh, and making the sale is the best part." She sounded dreamy, almost nostalgic. "Holdin' the cold hard cash in my hands, countin' the bills over and over, like they was endless." Then she jiggled. "Nothin' beats the feelin'."

He hadn't made a sale in months, not since he and Amelia arrived in Coolbeensia. They'd been busy trying to beat the obstacle course they had no intention of being on: first the time-sucking school, then the impossible exam, and now the hearing that would seal his fate. He hadn't had the time to devote to making a buck. Living off cash savings could only take them so far.

Peter kept his grip on the steering wheel as he focused on the road.

The long road to Unibrowumbia took them past miles and miles of swaying wheat fields, up and down rolling plains, and through wooded bottomlands. It was an hour's drive, but it seemed to take ages.

The quietness and gentle meandering over the peaks and valleys lulled Peter II to sleep in the backseat.

"Petey," Amelia said, breaking the silence, "about the hearing. Would the judge let you stay without me? You know, since we ain't married. Technically, you're the papa, but if the mama's in Unibrowumbia with it and you're in Coolbeensia alone, how's that go?"

The scenery whirred past like a blur as Peter kept his foot pressed on the gas.

His eyes narrowed. "Peter Losor ain't stayin' put nowhere without his woman and his son."

A relaxed smile crossed Amelia's plump face. Bobbing her head, she looked through the passenger side window and into the vastness of infinity.

At once the bright blue sky turned a drab gray. Menacing clouds swirled above like a wild sea on the brink of a vicious storm, ready to sink any foolhardy ship that dared to pass through. Short cracks of thunder sounded in the distance. It was as if the terrifying conditions foretold a grim future.

Amelia jumped. "It's gettin' scary." She wrapped her arms around herself. "And cold. Brr. Maybe I shoulda just stayed in Coolbeensia."

Peter shook his head. "The judge granted your voluntary departure. You ain't goin' back so soon. He ain't gonna be too happy if you did. It could jeopardize my case. Then we'll never get to stay."

She sighed and looked out of the window again. "You're right."

As the sky darkened and clouds twisted and swirled in a maniacal show of invincible power, an atmosphere of night descended upon them. But it was only early afternoon.

Peter II started to cry.

Amelia turned around. "Oh, shush!"

"Maybe he's hungry. Give him his bottle."

She reached into a cloth bag in the back seat, pulled out a bottle, and put in in the baby's car seat.

He cried louder.

Amelia turned to Peter pulling at his arm. "It won't keep quiet."

"Did you give him the bottle?"

"I did. I put the bottle right there in his car seat." She pointed to the back seat, although Peter kept his eyes on the road. The gloomy atmosphere didn't make for easy driving.

"You're supposed to put it in his hands so he knows it's there."

"Oh, oops."

Amelia reached again toward the back and placed the bottle in their son's tiny hands. He grabbed it instantly and began to drink.

She turned around with a clap, wiping her hands clean. "There, every time it cries, I'll give it a bottle. That'll shut it up."

Peter grumbled.

He soon turned into a parched lot with ground that appeared cracked in a thousand places. It looked like there'd been a drought. A lone farmhouse stood on the lot with the roof nearly caved in, a light green sheet for the front door, and exterior wooden boards warping from the merciless heat of many summers. Not a soul was around, neither neighbor nor animal. The only signs of life darted through the gloomy sky. The cawing of hungry crows, midnight black from beak to tail, and the *pit-peet* of western flycatchers made Amelia jump.

"This is Fred's old house?" she asked, gazing at the lonesome property.

Peter rolled up his window and opened the driver's-side door. "Yep."

He grabbed Amelia's things and instructed her to get the baby. "Looks like it's gonna rain. This place sure needs it." He kicked at the dry dirt before pulling the sheet to the side and entering the house.

He scanned the interior. "It's just like he left it."

The faded green wallpaper peeled, appearing as if someone's or some animal's claws had ripped it lengthwise. A layer of dust covered the work and kitchen tables. Dented metal pots and pans littered the kitchen countertops. An upholstered recliner sat next to the window that'd been partially barred up.

Amelia looked around with her mouth gaping open.

Peter tucked his hands into his jeans pockets and bounced on his toes. "Looks like you're gonna have to do some cleanin'."

He leaned over and pinched the back seat of the floral recliner that seemed to have survived at least a century. "Well, at least you got your own recliner." He pointed across the room. "And look, a rocking chair." He took a seat on it and slapped his hands on the armrests. "Classic. Creaky and everything."

His girlfriend stood speechless.

"Yep. Good ol' Fred lived here with his pack of dogs. Five Dobermans and one bullmastiff. The place wasn't big enough for all of 'em, so he up and moved out."

"Eww, dogs," Amelia said with a curl of her lips. Chewed-up dog beds, water bowls flipped upside down, worn collars, and crates were strewn around the house.

Peter stood up and clapped his hands. "Okay, you good?"

Amelia nodded slowly.

"All righty then. I'll be on my way."

He put his big hands on Amelia's arms and looked her in the eyes. "Now, you promise me you'll keep our son alive. You hear? This case should wrap up soon. Once I win, I'll come get you and him."

She rested her hand on his. "Don't you worry about nothin'. If we can survive anything, it'll survive anything. After all, it's a Losor and a Bord! It's got our fightin' genes."

Peter smiled and turned to go.

As he walked to his car, he couldn't help but wonder about his son. His girlfriend was right though. Peter II was a Losor-Bord. He had the pluck to withstand anything.

A sharp clap of lightning rattled him to the bone.

Chapter 31

A month later, Mila swerved into the courthouse parking lot at seven o'clock in the morning—three hours before Peter's third scheduled hearing. The lot was three-quarters full. Other spectators had the same idea: to grab a seat inside the courtroom before anxious Coolbeensians packed it chock-full.

She found a spot in the front of the gallery, giving her a clear view of where the plaintiff would stand. It'd give her uncommon satisfaction to see Peter, her Coolbeensian archenemy, whimper as the judge knocked him off his very unstable high horse. Quietly anticipating the deliverance of his just rewards, she brought out her phone and scrolled through the national news as she waited for the case to begin.

At 9:49 a.m., Peter pushed his way through the thick courtroom crowd, yelling, "Outta my way! Come on, I got a big hearing to get to," as he made his way to the counsel table.

Mila turned to look behind. Peter certainly didn't win anyone over with his world-class rudeness.

Despite wearing a sweater vest and faded jeans, he appeared noticeably different. He'd made the effort to be cleanly shaven, a major first, as he left a trail of cheap men's aftershave. Mila sniffed the air. Ah, the rancid smell of a dying skunk. It should've been illegal to wear. Nothing suited Peter better. He wore a smug smile and, stepping wide and swinging his arms, looked more confident than usual.

Mila was ready for the judge to tear Peter down, especially after the fiasco at the last hearing. Judge Eloney would rule in favor of Coolbeensia and the law requiring a parental license wouldn't change. Peter would hopefully be deported, and she'd feel safer starting her family in the company of other conscientious, licensed Coolbeensian parents.

The courtroom thrummed with constant chatter, mostly about speculations of how the case would set a legal precedent and a few whisperings about fleeing across the border to the foreign territory, Colorado, if it ended poorly.

Judge Eloney appeared and the hearing promptly started.

Mila sat without crossing her legs, as the gallery was too jam-packed for even slight movement. But she did have room to bounce her toes. Almost breathless, she kept her ears perked.

"Animal," Peter burst out with a hotheaded smile.

Spectators in the gallery glanced at each other, as if looking for logical answers they'd never find.

Mila bit her bottom lip. It was an unusual way to start the hearing. But then again, it was Peter who was at the plaintiff's table. He was capable of saying anything to anyone.

Judge Eloney stared at him for a minute with his jaw dropped. "Excuse me?"

"I'm an animal." Peter's tone came out deadpan, as if he had no speech filter.

What the devil was he up to?

"Mr. Losor, I realize that, and I do not argue with how you self-identify. But we are in a court of law, and you are expected to—"

Peter started scratching his side with one hand, raising his other arm over his head, and screeching, "Ooh-ooh ah-ah," like a monkey.

The gallery exploded in confused talk.

Mila felt a ringing in her ears. Was Peter really making monkey impressions in Coolbeensian court and expecting to be taken seriously? She had no answers for the life of her.

Judge Eloney pounded his gavel eight deafening times.

"Mr. Losor, do you realize you are in a courtroom and not in a wildlife zoo?"

Peter brought his arms to his side and stopped his outlandish impressions. "Of course, Your Honor, I do."

Mila smirked. What a smart aleck.

"Good. Now get to your point." The judge, with a grim twist of his mouth, sounded stern. "Today is your third and final hearing during which you have the opportunity to defend your stay here in Coolbeensia. We offer the accused due process when they allegedly violate the law. Please, now go on."

Peter took a deep breath as if preparing to give the dumbest defense yet. Still, he betrayed an air of confidence. He tilted back his head. "Your Honor, do you got animals in your micronation?"

Judge Eloney jerked his neck back and stammered. "Ye-yes, we do."

"What kind of animals? Dogs? Cats?"

"Well, yes, dogs and cats, as well as sheep and goats. We have them all," the judge replied.

Peter spoke deliberately, taking control.

Mila's muscles quivered.

"And do these animals procreate?" Peter asked.

"Of course they do. You know that. All animals give birth and have young'uns."

"And ain't these animals who have young'uns considered parents?" Holding his shoulders back and his chin high, Peter spoke with an escalating loudness that filled the courtroom. His voice full of bravado, he showed who had the upper hand.

Judge Eloney stammered again. "Uh, yes. Yes, they are."

No one in the courtroom looked like they knew where this was going, not even the flabbergasted judge.

"And do these animals, who are parents, need a parental license in Coolbeensia?" Peter asked.

Mila's mouth went dry.

"No, of course not." Judge Eloney's face and neck grew flushed. "Animals don't need a parental license at all!"

"And, Your Honor, ain't humans considered to be animals?"

A sensation of dread spread through Mila's frozen body.

"We're mammals—"

"And ain't mammals considered animals?"

"Ye-yes." The judge seemed cornered.

As her extremities went numb, Mila imagined the worst-case scenario.

"Then ain't it reasonable to conclude that since animals don't need no license, then humans, who ain't nothin' but animals, don't need no parental license either?"

The courtroom erupted in volatile exclamations of outrage as people flung their arms into the air.

Mila's chest caved in. She dropped her head into her hands, her fingers feeling icy to the touch.

Peter raised his brows, his eyes never veering from the judge. A smirk crossed his face.

This arrogant plaintiff wanted to laugh, didn't he?

The judge puffed out his cheeks, blowing out a long breath. Beads of sweat formed on his creased forehead as he rubbed it.

Who knew Peter could be so clever and leave the judge speechless?

Judge Eloney inhaled, then shut his eyes for a moment. When he opened them, he glanced around the gallery, where the spectators clasped their hands over their mouths, then moved them to their breastbone. Others kept a finger on their temples as they shook their heads.

Did they believe Peter? That Coolbeensian law was all wrong? Even worse, did Judge Eloney accept Peter's defense as truth?

Mila couldn't swallow. Her throat had grown tight.

Out of nowhere, a man burst out, "Peter's right! We don't need a license. It cost me my marriage!"

Mila turned her head. She knew that man. It was Tim, Vera's ex-husband. He'd failed the Parenthood Competency Test, and Vera divorced him partly because of it.

Then a woman from the back screamed, "He's got a book!"

Mila gasped and took cover behind the seat back.

Tim hurled the thick book at the judge. It flew across the courtroom and over Peter's head like a dangerous projectile. Judge Eloney ducked in time, just as the heavy book hit the Coolbeensian flag and sent it toppling.

The muscular bailiff threw himself on Tim, tackling him like a mean linebacker and bringing him crashing to the floor. His knee on his back, the bailiff handcuffed his hands behind him, then pulled him up and pushed him out of the courtroom.

Alarm filled the gallery from every angle.

Mila sat motionless amid the violence that had just taken took place. She wanted to escape the mounting tension and conflict, but nothing would persuade her to leave and not hear out this case. Not in its final days.

Once Tim no longer remained in the building, the courtroom gradually quieted.

"I'm all right," Judge Eloney reassured the spectators and the bailiff who'd returned.

Mila exhaled in relief.

"It's true, Coolbeensian law is known to make and break marriages, partnerships. But it's in the best interests of our youngest citizens."

He rearranged his blue robe and rubbed his face. He leaned over and reinstalled the Coolbeensian flag into the flag post at his side. "All is in order again. We shall proceed."

Peter didn't seem phased by the commotion. He stood there without a hint of fear on his face.

The judge cleared his throat.

Mila crossed her fingers and listened with a pounding heart.

"Mr. Losor, it is a fine argument you have presented. I commend you for your due diligence. But humans are a different kind of animal. We are reasoning animals, the only ones on Earth with the ability to differentiate right from wrong. Dogs and cats and sheep and goats do not possess the faculties of reason. Therefore, it is reasonable to conclude that human animals are held to a higher standard than farm animals, wild animals, and domesticated pets."

Peter's face flushed beet red.

He probably never saw that level of eloquence coming from Judge Eloney.

"Animals are not intentionally cruel to their young in the same way some unfortunate humans are toward their children. Animals act in survival mode, acting abusively or abandoning their young only under conditions where resources are limited and survival is paramount. Animals in general do not possess the wicked nature to abuse their own without reason.

"Humans are the only documented species to verbally or otherwise abuse their young—and this is the reason human parenting must be regulated."

A gladness filled Mila's heart. Eloney proved to be not only a likeminded friend who understood the complexities of human nature but an excellent judge who wielded the power to exercise social justice for all.

She breathed easier.

Chapter 32

At the one o'clock hour, strange clinking sounds awoke Peter. He popped his eyes open, listening on his side with his cheek resting on his hands. The *clink, clank* hammering noises came from near the front door.

The night was pitch black, thick and still. Nothing stirred, not even a crow or a mouse.

The only sound was the unexplainable one.

Peter wiped his clammy hands on his plaid boxer shorts.

He threw off the covers and crept through his darkened apartment. The clanking noises sounded like metal scraping against metal. He paused to listen. It did come from the front door, specifically the deadbolt lock. Someone was trying to break in!

He gulped down breaths, trying to stay silent. Ever since he began defending his natural human rights in court, he'd become a sort of local sensation. People packed the courthouse at each hearing, arching their necks to hear his every word. It wouldn't have been unusual to assume that someone had it in for him—someone who'd determined he shouldn't be in Coolbeensia.

His limbs started to shake, and his stomach felt rock hard.

He wouldn't go down, not without a fight.

Peter tiptoed to the kitchen, quietly pulled open the cupboard, and grabbed the handle of a sticky twelve-inch cast-iron pan. Wielding his makeshift weapon, he maneuvered stealthily toward the front door and held his breath.

He steadied himself, grasping the pan handle like a baseball bat. Standing in front of the closed door, he yanked it open with one hand and lifted his other arm, ready to bash the intruder's head.

"Petey!" came a familiar, whiny female voice.

"Wha?" Peter squinted his eyes, trying to see in the darkness. He made out a large shadowy figure, round like a life-size softball and a few inches shorter than him.

"Amelia?"

"Petey, I missed you," his girlfriend cried out.

Peter shuffled back a few steps as she threw her arms around him in a bear hug, then returned her embrace. He flicked on the light. "What're you doing here?"

He rubbed his stubbly face with his hand. It wasn't a psychopath or a determined petite suburban mom who wanted to take him out. It was only Amelia.

"Oh, I just hopped on a bus, comin' to check on ya." She gave him a playful poke in his beer belly, protruding from under his tank top. "You know, suprisin' ya, makin' sure no other woman snatched you up."

Peter groaned. "You came all this way to test my fidelity?"

"Fidelity? I don't play no fidelity."

He rolled his eyes. "Not fiddle. I'm talkin' about being faithful."

"Ooh. Well, you are a stud, you big ol' love bug."

She gave his arm a pinch.

"Ow!" He rubbed his now-painful arm. "Stop that."

The couple fell into a heated argument about how Amelia shouldn't have come just to make sure he wasn't cheating on her. He'd never do such a terrible thing, even if the ladies threw themselves at him. He paused to wonder why they never did. He shook his jowls. He didn't give it a second thought, since the most stunning ladies didn't know a good man when they saw one. Not that he noticed any of them.

Upon reconciling, Peter looked at his girlfriend's empty arms. He glanced at her feet, not seeing what he expected to see—no car seat, no bag, no bottle. He didn't hear what he thought he should hear: crying, whimpering, maybe a giggle.

"Where's our son?" he demanded, with a wildness encircling him.

"Oh, don't you worry your little head off about it. It's back in Unibrowumbia. I put it in the dog crate."

"You what?" Peter's eyes bulged like a madman's.

"Yeah, I put a big fat padlock on it to make sure it don't go nowhere. I even left it a milk bottle." Amelia smiled, as if she'd accomplished a great motherly thing.

Completely clueless, she yapped on and on, digging herself and him into a deeper grave.

Heat shot threw Peter's body the more she yammered.

"I found handcuffs layin' around." She made a dismissive wave with her hand. "But they was too big."

Peter's face grew as red as a fiery pepper, and steam practically blew out of his hairy ears. He took on the guise of a massive volcano in the midst of a catastrophic eruption, its boiling lava spewing thousands of feet into the air and inching steadily down his body, incinerating everything daring to be on its path.

He grabbed Amelia by the hand and yanked her out the door.

"Where we goin'?"

"Back to Unibrowumbia," he thundered.

Peter jumped into his rusty Chevy, with Amelia in the front seat, and floored the gas pedal. He raced past the border and toward the desolate enemy micronation.

It was no leisurely drive like those prior. Bolting down the highway, clocking Indy 500 racecar speeds of 170 miles per hour, Peter arrived at the farmhouse in forty minutes. His adrenaline pumping, he flew out of the driver's seat, leaving the engine running and Amelia shouting at him that nothing at all was wrong.

He couldn't breathe in enough oxygen as he pulled aside the sheet covering the front door.

He exhaled loudly as his son lay sleeping peacefully inside the dog crate, sucking his thumb and clutching a dog toy with the polyester fiber fill poking out. The padlock secured the crate, just as Amelia had said. He tore off the lock and grabbed his son.

Carrying him, he returned to his car and put Peter II in the car seat in the back.

"Where are you taking it?" Amelia cried out.

"Our son's stayin' with Geraldine," Peter grumbled, eyeing the road that would take him to his cousin's house, just five miles from Fred's old farmhouse.

In no time, he arrived at Geraldine's home and knocked thrice on the front door. All the lights were out, being three o'clock in the morning. Peter paced back and forth with his son still sleeping in his arms.

Tension grew in his neck and shoulders when no one answered.

After a few minutes of shuffling inside and a light flicking on, Geraldine opened the door in the midst of tying her pink cotton robe. Plastic pink curlers wove tightly in her chestnut hair, her gaunt face appeared pale in the darkness.

"Peter, what're you doin' here so early in the mornin'?" she asked, wide-eyed.

"Geraldine, I need a favor. Can you watch my son for a while? I got some business to take care of."

"Sure. You talkin' about your *business* business?" she asked with a wink.

"Nah, I got somethin' else." He handed her Peter II and ran back to his car. "I owe you one, Geraldine!"

Amelia sat waiting in the vehicle, twiddling her thumbs.

"What about me?" she asked.

"You're gonna stay here."

"In Unibrowumbia?"

"Yeah," he growled, driving her back to the old farmhouse. He left her there and rushed back to Coolbeensia, careful to reenter through the unsecured opening in the border.

Upon reaching his apartment after a long hour of treacherous, sleepy driving and nearly veering off the road three times, he collapsed in bed. It was almost 4:30 in the morning—four-and-a-half hours before the final hearing, when the judge would give his ruling and seal his fate.

He didn't have the time or energy to dwell on it. Dealing with his witless girlfriend had disrupted what should've been a restful night, one that would've prepared him for what was soon to come.

Peter snatched only a few hours of shut-eye before he had to rouse himself up again and drag himself to the courthouse. Losing valuable sleep didn't help. Furthermore, his chaotic night did nothing to improve his state of mind—and he needed a good one to face his uncertain future.

Chapter 33

Mila had camped out on the courthouse lawn the night before the ruling, along with dozens of other eager spectators. She'd hauled along all the essentials: pretzels, an egg sandwich, water bottles, a chair, and a jacket. The group had lit a small bonfire and chatted, cried, and laughed on the grass until well past midnight about how they'd anticipated the case might turn out.

Bright and early on judgment day, Mila stretched her arms and swigged her cold coffee from her thermos. She unzipped her tent and peeked out, seeing nearby houses with carved jack-o'-lanterns grinning on their porches, decals of flying bats stuck to their windows, and the trees bursting with bright orange, red, and yellow foliage.

The morning breeze blew cool and fresh. She inhaled deeply, ready more than ever to learn the final resolution that would either put her on a clean, direct path to parenthood or force her to start her family in a safer place that aligned with her high ideals.

She rolled up her blanket and stuffed it and her tent into the trunk of her car. Then she strolled into the courtroom.

Despite it being six o'clock, the gallery was already half full.

She took a seat up front, tapping her feet and repeatedly glancing at the clock for the next three hours.

At approximately 8:45 a.m., Peter sauntered in hunched over with his eyes half closed, resembling a ghoulish zombie straight out of a horror flick. One leg of his jeans had rolled up revealing his hairy ankle. He fit in perfectly with the month's Halloween theme.

He staggered to the counsel desk, plopped down, and dozed off.

It was just like Peter to fall asleep on the day of the judge's ruling. Mila let out a quick, disgusted snort. He couldn't be expected to show respect to himself or anyone else. Hopefully the judge wouldn't be swayed by Peter's past arguments and see the necessity of Coolbeensia's most famous law.

The noise in the courtroom grew clamorous with people talking and laughing as if they were at an outdoor movie. Given Peter's showmanship, the hearing did carry high entertainment value. Mila turned her head to get an idea of the number of spectators in the courtroom. Her posture stiffened.

Thousands of spectators spilled out of the courtroom, with lines extending beyond the front door. People packed the front lawn, took up every inch of standing room in the parking lot, and flocked to the nearby roads. The courthouse door couldn't close due to the congested crowds hoping to catch a glimpse of what would become the most famous ruling in Coolbeensia history.

Judge Eloney took his place at the bench.

Peter's head still rested on his left shoulder—and he snored, obnoxiously loud.

At precisely nine o'clock, the bailiff called for order in the court and the hearing started.

"Mr. Losor, while sleeping in the court is not against the law, your snoring is disruptive," the judge said.

Peter didn't stir.

"Mr. Losor!" the judge shouted. He pounded his gavel five times, producing thunderous *bangs* that were probably heard around the block.

Peter startled awake. "Hu-huh? Oh, hey, Your Honor." He gave a weak smile.

"Don't you start snoring again, Mr. Losor, or you will be held in contempt of court."

"Nah, of course not, Your Honor. I wouldn't fall aslee—"

His head dropped to his shoulder again.

And he started snoring.

With another bang of his gavel, Judge Eloney shouted, "That's it. You are held in contempt of court and fined one hundred brincadors!"

At the mention of brincadors, Peter bolted awake. He blinked a few times and scratched his head, as if to determine where he was. He was undeniably in the middle of his own self-created nightmare.

Mila crossed her arms and smirked.

"It's nice to see you awake, Mr. Losor. I've listened to your arguments over the past three hearings. After much deliberation, I have arrived at what I consider to be a fair judgement."

The skin around Peter's eyes tightened.

Mila leaned forward with a flutter in her stomach.

Utter silence crushed the loud courtroom noise of the five minutes prior.

Judge Eloney glanced around at the spectators and cleared his throat.

"Let me start by saying that upon birth, a contract is automatically created between you and the child. You and your girlfriend entered this automatic contract with your child once he was born. This obligates you to fulfill the terms of the contract, which include raising him with love and care until he is ready to care for himself.

"I understand people describe what constitutes love and care differently. Here in Coolbeensia, we define love and care as that which helps a child develop in the healthiest way. Part of that love and care is first proving you can be a responsible parent by earning a license.

"Furthermore, the length of the contract is clear—eighteen years. Had you paid attention in class, you would've learned that. By not obtaining a parental license, you fail to honor your end of the deal."

Peter's bottom lip quivered as he stood facing the judge. He seemed, for once, almost helpless.

Judge Eloney expanded upon his opinion. "Having a child is easy elsewhere in the world, which explains a lot of the misfortunes and maladies. But here in Coolbeensia, the road to parenthood is long and arduous—on purpose. You see, Mr. Losor, that which comes after great difficulty is valued even more.

"I'm talking about children." He made strong eye contact with Peter. "If children weren't as easily begotten as socks, or batteries, or other everyday consumer goods, their parents would hold them more preciously."

Peter stood like a soldier, not twitching a muscle.

Mila nodded as her smile reached her eyes.

"Coolbeensian law serves to protect the most vulnerable, who have no say in who their parents are. A child could be fortunate and be born into a loving family. Or a luckless child may be the offspring of ill-fitting parents who don't have a clue about how to raise a dependent, much less well.

"But Coolbeensian law does not leave this up to chance. We impose strict measures to best ensure that the wee ones brand new to the world have every opportunity to receive life-affirming love and care."

Mila felt the urge to applaud, but she sided with courtroom etiquette and suppressed her joy. She'd have all the reason to clap once it was all over—she was sure of it. She was a smidgeon close to hearing the final verdict she'd wanted to hear ever since this nonsense took over her life.

"Coolbeensian law shapes parents' behaviors. Earning a parental license shows their commitment to their role and guides them in their parenting journey. It goes a long way in preventing misconduct from happening in the first place. Licensed parents are more conscientious parents."

Peter hung his head.

Defeat emanated out of every pore in his body.

Judge Eloney looked sternly at Peter. "You have not persuaded me that a Coolbeensian parent does not need a license. Therefore, your punishment, which is long overdue, is in order. You will be fined seven hundred brincadors, one hundred for each month you've remained an unlicensed parent. You will also be sentenced to nine months in jail.

"You will carry out your sentence in our one-room jailhouse, which is currently occupied by another individual. He literally threw the book at me, and I've metaphorically thrown the book at him. That gentleman, Tim Maybena, will be your cellmate. Pay heed, Mr. Losor. We have been very lenient with you. If you still fail to become licensed after serving your sentence, you will be deported."

The judge hammered his gavel.

"Case dismissed."

A burst of warmth radiated through Mila, from the top of her head to the tips of her toes. She placed her palm against her chest as tears rolled down her face. She exhaled. The outcome was just.

Spectators in the courtroom leaped to their feet, applauding wildly. Hoots and hollers were heard from outside the courthouse as news of the judgment spread like wildfire.

Mila wanted to run to the bench and give Eloney a big hug. His judgment preserved the most compassionate law in human history. Her dear friend gave her the confidence to stay and start her family in this quaint but joyous micronation.

Two minutes later, she received a text from Jason. He'd seen the outcome of the case streaming on multiple news channels all over Coolbeensia.

"So maybe now we can start making a baby?"

Mila threw her head back and laughed.

Chapter 34

"Here's to us, future parents!" Jason said.

"Without anything left to stop us!" Mila added, raising her fluted glass.

Their arms entwining around each other's, Mila and Jason sipped glasses of sparkly, sweet pinot noir.

Mila licked her lips and admired the ruby-colored champagne swirling in her glass. "Mm. The raspberry leaves a delicious, velvety softness on my palate."

The candles on the table delivered a comforting warmth, and the half-filled champagne flutes glowed under the candlesticks' flickering flames. Mila closed her eyes and lifted her nose to breathe in the honey-like scents wafting from the bouquet of red roses Jason had given her.

She dug her fork into a homecooked dinner of tender scallops drenched in rich pesto cream sauce. It was a sumptuous dinner celebrating the victorious court ruling earlier that morning.

"Hon, you added just the right amount of hot pepper. Not too spicy, but just right," Mila said about her husband's delectable preparation.

"Some do like it hot." Jason gave her a wink.

Mila shivered with anticipation. With the drama and distractions behind her, she longed to be closer to her husband.

She snuffed out the candles. Jason led her by the hand as they ended their celebratory night in the bedroom.

"Shall we say, 'let the celebrations begin?'" Mila asked, letting herself free fall on the luxury down comforter with Jason following suit.

They cuddled and giggled and laughed all through the endless night.

One early morning ten days later, Mila shrieked. Her pulse raced and her neck grew flushed.

Dropping his smartphone, Jason rushed to the bathroom, where his wife stood in the doorway holding a pregnancy test.

With a big grin on her face, she squealed, "We're pregnant!"

Meanwhile, Peter fled Coolbeensia. Nobody was about to put him back in jail. He'd had enough of living as a fugitive behind bars. A man like him needed freedom. He had a business to run, and he couldn't do it from a jail cell—he wasn't *that* well-connected.

He hurried to Fred's house first and was met with the low growling of his cousin's guard dogs. "Down boy, down. Don't you recognize me? It's Peter." He threw his arms up in the air to avoid getting bitten.

Fred emerged from the house, likely after hearing all the commotion in his front yard.

"Hey, Fred, where are the guns?" Peter didn't dillydally.

Fred, standing six-foot tall and lean, replied in a monotone voice, as if he were used to hearing pointed questions, "Guns? We barely got money to buy sandwiches. How we gonna buy guns?"

"Oh, right. Never mind."

"What d'ya need guns for anyway?"

"Coolbeensia been givin' me trouble. They wanna put me in jail."

Fred's left eyebrow went up. "Them too? What for, the usual?"

"Nah, it's for an even stupider reason. I ain't got no parental license. That's why."

"A what?"

"A professional parenting license," Peter replied, raising his voice. "That's what they call it."

"Hmm. Okay, whatever." Fred stuck his hands into his jean pockets and gazed out over the rugged, reddish landscape.

"I need to get Unibrowumbia together. Where's Georgie?"

"Um, he's at the pond, fishin'."

"Good. I'm headin' over there. See ya." Peter rushed back to his Chevy and drove over the rolling hills toward the pond. He parked on the dirt, leaving fat tire tracks in his wake.

Georgie had a line thrown out. He leaned back against the bark of an oak tree with his straw hat covering his eyes.

Peter moseyed up. "Hey, Georgie!"

The old man stirred. He pushed the rim of his hat up and looked to where the voice had come from. "Hey, Petey! Long time no see. What brings ya to these parts?"

Peter sat down on the grass next to his old friend. Georgie used to take him fishing when he was ten, the only grownup who'd ever paid him any attention. He was like an uncle to Peter, the wisest Unibrowumbian he'd ever met, made better with a wicked sense of humor.

"Listen, Georgie, since you the president of Unibrowumbia, I need a favor."

"Oh, oh, what can I do fer ya?" His voice crackled, as if he'd spent hours by the pond not speaking to a soul.

"I need you to wage war against Coolbeensia. And I need all the chili peppers Unibrowumbia's got."

"War?" He scratched his head.

"Yep. We ain't got no guns, no tanks, no grenades, nothin'. So, I gotta improvise."

"Whatcha gonna do, wage chili pepper warfare?"

"That's exactly what I'm gonna do." Peter narrowed his eyes and rubbed his hands together.

"Someone musta really teed you off for ya to go about the business of chili pepper warfare."

"Yeah, they sure did." Venting his woes, Peter felt a release of tension. "They made me real mad, talkin' about throwin' me in jail for havin' no stupid license. Parents don't need no license. I'm proof." He pointed to himself with both his thumbs.

"Oh, now you in big trouble. Well, we got tons of chilis: pits of dried chilis and chili fields with chili flowers that're 'bout to spring some brand-new chilis. You welcome to help yerself." Georgie looked up at him with his weathered face and toothless smile.

"Thanks, Georgie." He patted his friend on the back. "I knew I could count on you."

Peter hurried back to his Chevy and spun the steering wheel, heading toward the pits.

All night, he ground up the dried chilis into a fine powder, then sealed them in containers filled with water. Everyone he knew growing up in Unibrowumbia owned water guns. He'd lead this war with all his friends, family, and the community fighting with him, water guns in hand, ready to shock enemy Coolbeensians with burning sprays of chili pepper juice.

Which is exactly what he did the next day.

Chapter 35

Peter organized the Unibrowumbia residents, young and old, foolhardy and more foolhardy, weak and strong. Throngs of citizens pulled up to the Coolbeensian border in their rickety, hissing cars just as the sun rose. Each passenger carried a plastic water gun filled with Peter's homemade chili juice.

Upon his instruction, they discharged their weapons, hurling stinging chili juice at every passing Coolbeensian. The residents screamed, shielded their faces, and ran for cover.

Within one minute, a bystander informed President Eloney that their micronation was being attacked by Unibrowumbians. At their lead was Peter Losor, recognizable from the court case that drew national attention.

Immediately, President Eloney positioned himself on his lime-green recliner with his smartphone on a tripod. He streamed an urgent announcement to his people.

"My fellow citizens, residents of Coolbeensia, I must make a dire announcement. Our micronation is in the presence of great danger. We are under attack by Unibrowumbian aggressors. We consider ourselves in a state of war due to their heinous acts. As your commander in chief, vested with the full powers of the Coolbeensian army, navy, and air force, I promise to protect each and every one of us."

Mila watched the president's declaration of war on her smartphone, shaking her head.

"Did you hear that?" she asked Jason, sitting in the next chair.

"I did—"

A second later, Mila had grabbed her jacket and swung open the front door.

"Where are you going?"

"I need to see Eloney!" She raced out.

Her drive to the presidential mansion took less than five minutes, as she didn't take her foot off the gas.

Margaret opened the front door, cupping her hands over her mouth. Her eyes welling up with tears, she pointed to the living room.

Mila hurried there, finding Eloney putting away his tripod.

"Eloney!" She grabbed him by the elbow. "I thought you said Coolbeensia had an army and a navy and an air force!"

"Of course we have proper defenses. Our naval fleet, consisting of fifteen inflatable rafts, serves as a major deterrent to aggression around the micronation."

Mila's eyes became glassy as she shrank back.

"Our marine corps maintains twenty-five amphibious frogs for combat operations."

Mila covered her open mouth with her hand.

"We've got a proud air force with rapid air space capability." He bounced on his toes. "We're also equipped with military arms."

"Why don't you counterattack with military arms?" she asked, her hands trembling.

"We'll try. Our military arms consist of love and peace and reconciliation, which protect our micronation from aggressors."

"They consist of *what*?" Mila almost choked on her own words.

"Love and reconciliation. They're powerful when used right."

Eloney didn't seem at all concerned about his choice of defense capabilities.

Mila smacked her forehead with her palm.

"Coolbeensia has never been at war. We've remained a peaceful micronation from the start. This is our very first war. I'm sure we'll defeat the enemy with our fine defenses." He gave her a grandfatherly smile.

For goodness' sake, she was pregnant and in the middle of a war! Her maternal instincts, intensified by her rising hormones, kicked in. She was a ferocious mama tiger, ready to protect her unborn baby no matter how high the cost.

She lunged toward Eloney, grabbed him by the collar, and screamed in his face, "Coolbeensia's defenses are frogs, inflatable rafts, love, and reconciliation?"

"Calm down, Mila."

He looked a little scared.

She stepped back and took a deep breath. "Okay, okay. We're being attacked with chili pepper juice. We need to act." She stomped her foot. "And fast."

"I've already called for supports."

"What supports?"

"Well, we've got an annual hot air balloon festival here every June, and our good friends there have agreed to lend us their hot air balloons."

Hot air balloons?

Mila went cross-eyed.

Over the next few days, Coolbeensian citizens went to work filling hundreds of balloons with a mix of soap and water. Then they inflated several hundred more balloons with laughing gas.

Upon climbing into the hot air balloons with their makeshift weapons, they soared the dark skies over Unibrowumbia.

"Fire!" they shouted.

At once, the Coolbeensians dropped the balloons. As the soap bombs burst open upon hitting the ground, the enemy cars skidded over the soapy roadways, colliding, piling up, and barricading the way so that their cars couldn't pass through.

As the fighting raged on, Peter handed Amelia a water gun filled with chili juice. "Here, fire this whenever you see a Coolbeensian. And teach our son how to pull the trigger."

"But it ain't even able to hold a bottle right!" Amelia complained.

"He's gotta learn to use a gun. He's a Losor-Bord. Do what you can." Peter rushed off to the battlefield.

The blockade of cars prevented more Unibrowumbians from entering Coolbeensia.

Seeing the car wreckages near the border, Mila raced to the frontlines. She found herself face-to-face with the enemy himself: Peter Losor. She wasn't about to let him win this fateful war.

Peter aimed his water gun straight at Mila.

Her muscles tightened as she gripped a balloon filled with laughing gas. "You'll never topple the great

Coolbeensia!" she cried out, hurling it at him just as he pulled the trigger.

Mila spun her body to avert the stinging spray of chili juice.

Then she heard a loud thud. Peter had collapsed to the ground, laughing like a lunatic. Mila's shoulders relaxed. The laughing gas made him too loopy to fight.

Amid the frenzy of piled-up cars, Unibrowumbians amusingly slipping and falling, and the unfortunate adversaries curled up laughing and clutching their stomachs, Georgie stood at the border solemnly waving a white flag.

Coolbeensian citizens captured Unibrowumbia's defeat on their smartphones.

Moments later, President Eloney streamed his victory speech.

Letting out a huge exhale, Mila pressed a hand to her heart and, with her other, patted her belly.

Chapter 36

Mila smoothed out the panda-print fitted sheet in the baby crib. She and Jason had just purchased a brand-new single-family home, complete with a large master bedroom, a guest room, and a room for their coming bundle of joy. Zebra, giraffe, and lion decals covered one wall in the baby's room. On the adjacent wall stood a carved wooden sculpture in the shape of a tree, its branches serving as shelves for picture books, stuffed animals, and baby outfits.

She glanced at the plain, white wall next to the crib and tilted her head.

"Hmm. Looks a bit crooked." She reached out to straighten the polished mahogany wood frame that held her parental license. "There, all better."

The license was the only form of décor that hung on the wall above the crib. It couldn't be missed, was clearly legible, and served a fundamental purpose. No matter how life turned out—and life had all sorts of bizarre twists and turns—her forthcoming child would grow up knowing their parents did everything they could to foster a wonderful, happy childhood.

Then the *ding dong!* of the grandfather clock sounded. It was already noon.

Mila yelled out, "Jason, we better get going!"

"Coming, hon."

Vera was throwing her a baby shower, which included some very important guests. Jason's and Mila's parents flew in from foreign territories, specifically Florida and Delaware. She'd advised them to bring their passports, as they'd need to clear customs and immigration. Vera had set up an area for video calls so that any of her friends or relatives without valid passports could still be a part of the celebrations.

Jason buttoned the top two buttons of his casual shirt as he slid into his slip-on shoes.

While adjusting the heel, he met his wife's gaze. "Honey, you look beautiful."

Mila, in her airy, floral print, off-the-shoulder dress, rubbed her big belly. At eight months pregnant, she felt beautiful, even radiant.

"Thanks, hon."

They drove to the community park, all set up with picnic blankets and cushions laid out on the lush green grass, pink and blue balloons near the trimmed hedges, and twisting streamers lining the pavilions.

It was the perfect June day with clear blue skies, a sun that lent generous warmth, and not a rain cloud in sight. Vera took Mila by the hands as soon as she arrived.

"Vera, you'll be next," Mila joked.

"I'm hoping," Vera said. "Bao and I are trying!"

The refreshment table looked appetizing, with tables heaping with pastel blue marshmallow rattles loaded with shimmery silver sprinkles, crips diaper pastries with luscious strawberry filling oozing out, a square cheese block with letters of the alphabet decorating all four sides, and purple-colored berry smoothies served in old-fashioned milk bottles.

Mila helped herself to a plate of crackers and cheese.

As she cut a second slice, Simon ambled up carrying a plate of blue cloud cookies.

"Simon!" Mila put one arm around her old study group friend.

"You finally passed, didn't you?"

Beaming, he nodded.

"Oh, I'm so happy for you."

"I'd like you to meet Alyssa, my new girlfriend." Simon gestured to the demure young woman next to him.

"Nice to meet you." Mila reached out and gave her a light hug.

"I've been tutoring her on the Parenthood Competency Test." Simon gave his girlfriend an awkward sideways glance and, looking down at his shifting feet, grinned a silly grin. "We're getting serious."

"He'll be the kindest baby father you could ever hope for," Mila said to Alyssa.

As the couple moved down the refreshment table, Mila's parents strolled up with red drink cups.

Mr. Petrov pointed his finger at his daughter's large belly. "Our legacy is in that baby bump, right there!"

Mrs. Petrov leaned down to eye level with her daughter's baby bump. "Babies may not be born with instructions, but rest assured, little girl or boy, your parents are fully licensed."

Mila caressed her round stomach, just as Jason walked up with his parents.

"Good thing grandparents don't need a license, huh?" the elder Mr. Winston said.

"Well," replied Mila, "if you lived in Coolbeensia . . ."

Everyone in the family threw their heads back in jovial laughter.

The festivities rolled on. Before long, it was time to open the presents.

Mila stepped over to the gift table, topped with a range of ginormous and tiny boxes, all neatly wrapped in pastel gift wrap and sparkly bows.

"Are you having a girl or a boy?" one of the guests asked.

"We don't know yet. Jason and I aim to find out on his or her *birth* day!" Mila squealed. "However our little baby chooses to come out, it'll be love at first sight."

She began unwrapping her assortment of gifts. She'd receive too many stuffed animals to count, a soft muslin foodie swaddle in an avocado print, a practical baby starter set that included tiny pajamas and a cozy sleep sack, a mini trolley for the months when the baby takes off running across the living room, a baby sound machine to soothe her wee one to sleep, and a must-have changing table kit.

"Wait, there's one more!" Vera pointed to the parking lot, where a giant plush dog with a black-and-white polka-dot bow sat in the back of Bao's pickup truck.

Mila slapped her hands against her cheeks.

After she expressed her appreciation to her guests, the event wound down. Mila and Jason returned home with the giant plushie poking its furry head out of their backseat car window.

Jason placed it in the corner of the baby room.

Mila straightened up the stuffed dog's giant bowtie. "Maybe I ought to work with Eloney on legislation for pet parent licensure too. Huh, hon?" she mentioned half joking.

"I'd be amazed at anything you set out to do."

One uneventful sunny morning late in June, Mila opened her email. In her inbox was a message from the Coolbeensian Professional Parent Guild.

Upon opening and reading the email, she jumped off the couch, hollering.

Jason hurried to the living room, rubbing the hairs that had straightened up on the back of his neck. "Is it time? Is it time?"

Mila threw her hands into the air and ran a little victory lap around the living room. "No, it's not. But I've been accepted into the guild! It's great news!"

In the midst of dancing in place, she bowled over without warning, clutching her belly. Jason put his arms over his wife's shoulder to support her. "It's awesome news. But are you sure you're okay?"

Facing the carpet, Mila shook her head.

"My water. It just broke."

Jason gasped. "Okay, okay. I know what to do." He turned around and around in dizzying circles, scraping his hands through his hair. "I know what to do."

Between panting, Mila instructed, "Honey, to the hospital."

"Oh, right." He grabbed the baby bag at the front door and whisked it into the car.

"Wife." He turned around. "Mustn't forget the wife!"

He escorted Mila to the car and sped to the hospital.

Five hours later, Mila, drenched in sweat and tears, gave birth to a baby girl. She held her pride and joy with a tenderness she'd never known before. She was in heaven. Or rather, heaven cried nonstop in her arms. A beautiful mix of love, euphoria, and relief spread through every fiber of her being.

"We'll call her Celeste, because we live in the most heavenly nation on Earth."

Jason stood by her side in the birthing room, grinning as a proud new dad but, at the same time, with a little fear and panic in his eyes.

Mila glanced up at him. "Don't worry. You'll be an amazing father."

Cradling her daughter in her arms, she cried tears of joy. "We did it. We finally did it!"

And so they began their happy new lives as Coolbeensian parents. But they didn't stop at one child. Over the next six years, the couple added four more to their brood. The Winstons had joined the prestigious ranks of Coolbeensian parents: caring, responsible—and *licensed to rear*.

Thank you for reading *Licensed to Rear*. If you found this family fiction tale stimulating, please share your review at your favorite retailer. It'd be much appreciated!

www.riyapresents.com

Acknowledgements

I'd like to thank my editor, Sara DeGonia.
I'd also like to thank the legions of horrible parents around the world, without whom there would be no need to write this book.

www.ingramcontent.com/pod-product-compliance
Lightning Source LLC
Chambersburg PA
CBHW070913120626
46546CB00001B/240